MORE
Missions
Accomplished

…And a lot more funny business

Tim Jenkins

MORE MISSIONS ACCOMPLISHED

ISBN: 0999881538
ISBN-13: 978-0-9998815-3-8

This book describes the authors experiences while traveling – on the road, in the air, at sea and through life events – and reflects his opinions of those experiences. Some names and details have been changed to protect privacy, add cohesion, and to entertain.

If you enjoy <u>More Missions Accomplished</u>, please leave a review on Amazon and consider reading its predecessor, <u>Missions Accomplished</u>. Learn more about the author at: missionsaccomplishedpress.com

To First Responders
Those that saved our home and our city
During the Great Santa Rosa Firestorm of 2017
And everywhere around the world
There is always another mission
The good you do is forever

ACKNOWLEDGMENTS

This second book of Missions Accomplished again benefited from the excellent work and dedication of:

Carol Marks, Editor Extraordinaire
who not only fixes what's broken but questions everything that doesn't make sense – she had a lot of questions, and the book benefited from them all.

Heather Workman, Graphic Arts Magician
who follows instructions super well when they make sense and correctly disregards them when they don't.

My daughter, Michelle Samantha Jenkins
For cover photography, the use of her bunny, Larry, and her unerring ability to gently guide the author to the right answer every time.

And to my cadre of story critics – you know who you are – many of whom have traveled with me, and some still willing to do so again in the future.

Where to next?

CONTENTS

GANDHI MODE

MISSION MODE

Modes of Accomplishment

"History shall be kind to me, for I intend to write it."
-- Sir Winston Churchill

And he did, volumes of it. It *was* reasonably kind to him. That these Missions Accomplished stories comprise something of a personal history for me is a coincidental outcome, a by-product of their intended purpose, which is to educate and amuse the reader regarding my lessons learned while on the journey – for business, pleasure, and through life itself.

My approach here is a little different than Churchill's: these travel anecdotes and vignettes are true lessons learned, and oftentimes the learning process wasn't pretty.

I've found it's more rewarding to self-deprecate than to ballyhoo, though either behavior could be called self-absorbed, perhaps. "Write what you know," said Mark Twain. Travel blunders and misadventures, that's where I feel right at home.

Sometimes I had help in the form of colorful and mischievous travel companions. To the extent I can spare those who've journeyed with me, I'm eager to do so, but not to the point of dropping these wonderful characters from the narrative. The foolishness herein mostly indict the author. If you, the reader, can construct something of the author's flaws from these tales, more's the better. It shouldn't be hard.

Here you'll learn how to avoid being the most hated person on the Tokyo subway. Why it pays to keep smiling even when a stranger collapses into your lap while you're trying to snooze in your airline seat. You'll tangle with the dogs of the Taiwan Canine Customs Service, and enjoy a vigorous flogging in the frozen north of Finland. You'll be exposed to different cultures and some fascinating lands – like The Philippines, India, France, California, and even that mythically different place we Americans call "Our Nation's Capital" -- Washington, DC.

My elevator pitch of travel wisdom: stay on the trail, mostly, and don't slow down until the mission is accomplished. Most of all, enjoy every moment of the journey, however awkward. If it's not awkward sometimes, you're probably not doing it right.

Churchill said something else applicable here: "The pessimist sees difficulty in every opportunity. The optimist sees the opportunity in every difficulty." On the road, I've seen a lot of opportunity. Keep your eyes and your mind open, and you're apt to do likewise.

Happy travels!

CRUISE MODE

SHENZHEN, CHINA – 2009

The Best Fruit in Southern China

Just because you've been to KTV doesn't mean you can sing.

In came a young woman holding a tray containing two fancy crystal glasses, each with slices of melon, honeydew, and guava. A thin, silvery sundae spoon and colorful umbrella poked out of each. It looked very refreshing.

"Wow," said Blaze, "this is great! We didn't even order fruit."

The woman, who's name tag said "Mei Ling" in Chinese, gestured at the menus before us. We each picked one up. She made a motion like she was drinking from a cup and asked us what we wanted.

"Beer," I said.

Chardonnay," said Blaze.

Mei Ling shook her head and explained in Chinese. "Only one kind of drink."

The penny was dropping. I'd been to this kind of karaoke – a Japanese style sing-along club, often called KTV – many times before. It occurred to me now that I'd never walked into one without the guidance of a local host, however. And every time I'd been to one, my friends and I had been served the exact same drink. If beer was ordered, that was what everyone had to consume, with vast quantities inherent in the proposition.

The economics of just us two novices in a big karaoke room now struck me as problematic. "How much for white wine?" I asked. Mei Ling pointed back to the menu, which contained nothing like grape wine. Rather, it was beer – Heineken, to be exact – or hard liquor, whiskey, vodka, or gin, with which she demonstrated we would also get two clean glasses and a bowl of ice cubes, if we wanted. The price: 1500 RMB – more than $200 U.S.

That was just for beverages. "How much for singing?" 800 RMB to occupy the room, which was nicely upholstered, had a great sound system, and two microphones. The fruit was 600 RMB, and we would need to hire a DJ, to facilitate playing music without lyrics, to which Blaze and I would sing. Four hundred. Oh, and there was a caretaker fee, so that someone could come in and check on us to see how much more liquor and ice cubes we needed. That was another 400 RMB.

Total price: well over $500 dollars! We were out of our league.

Blaze stood. "Oh, sorry," he said, "perhaps another time."

Mei Ling would have none of it. "Please, sit down. Sit!"

"I think we must be going," I told her, just so there was no misunderstanding. But of course, there was. Before we could stride out of the room, she shot out like a bolt.

At the reception podium where we'd come in, Mei Ling was hurriedly explaining to her boss what was happening. He turned as we approached. "Wait," he said in English. "Pay the bill." And sure enough, he handed us a tab for 3300 RMB – full fare.

"We just sat down for five minutes," Blaze said. "We're not going to pay you anything."

"She says you ordered fruit," said the boss.

Blaze led the protest. "We didn't order any fruit. We didn't touch it, either. And now we're leaving. No fruit, no singing, no drinking. No money. B-b-b-bye!"

I knew it wouldn't be that easy, but he was on a roll. As we walked out, making a very big deal of waving goodbye – just to prevent misunderstanding -- more club personnel were assembling. We hit the sidewalk, and from behind us came the sound of running footsteps. Blaze trotted over to a waiting cab. There were three more behind it. We got in, and I hurriedly gave the driver our hotel card.

To no avail. The club staff, led by a now furious looking Mei Ling, were surrounding the cab. She leaned into the driver's window and shouted something about "these foreigners haven't paid! Don't take them anywhere."

He yelled back at her. But then he turned his hands up, the universal "nothing I can do" gesture. Perhaps he was concerned we wouldn't pay him, either, but I rather think he caved to peer pressure. Blaze thought he'd be clever by jumping into the cab right behind. I knew that wouldn't fly either. That driver was even less amiable. "No, you must get out." He informed us.

Blaze jumped out of the second cab and was confronted by a large man who was lecturing him and poking him in the chest with an index finger. That didn't go over well.

Blaze, smiling, took the man's finger and held it fast. "Don't touch me."

The man suddenly looked frightened. He tried to wriggle his finger away. Blaze gripped it firmly. "You don't have permission to touch anyone like that. You want me to give this finger back to you? Then you better apologize!" Blaze kept smiling, but he wasn't kidding.

The man wilted enough that Blaze let him go without the apology. Then Blaze strode down the sidewalk. I followed, and so did the entire club staff. They dogged our heels, haranguing us from behind. One of them started shouting for the police.

I turned. "You want the police?" I asked. "Yes, get them, since you are assaulting foreigners. The police will definitely want to talk to you." No more calls were made regarding police. Yet the chase continued. It was obvious we'd never get a taxi out of this part of town.

Blaze turned suddenly and shouted. "How much does the fruit cost? We'll pay for the fruit, but that's it!"

The man who'd poked Blaze now held out his arm and gestured for Blaze to take it. He pointed back to the club. Blaze, grinning, jauntily locked arms with him, and they began merrily striding together back toward the club.

It was a sight. Another club staffer, emboldened, tried to take Blaze's other arm. He was comprehensively rebuffed and belittled by Blaze, who broke from the first man and began waving his arms in a dominance gesture that no primate could ever mistake. The second man backed off, and Blaze resumed his giddy saunter arm-in-arm with Mr. Poke-a-Finger.

Back at the podium, I did the negotiating. "Fruit only. 600 RMB."

"And we get to eat the fruit," added Blaze. I thought this was going too far, but Mei Ling sprinted down the hall and brought the two crystal cups laden with fruit. Blaze made short work of them both, dripping juice on the floor and grinning, while I counted out the cash, equivalent to $85 back home.

"That's too much money for fruit!" I admonished the club owner.

Blaze put a hand on my shoulder. "Easy," he assuaged. "That was really good fruit."

This time, when we got in the cab, the club staff waved us adieu. The driver looked suspicious, but shrugged and pulled away from the curb.

"What say we try a different karaoke club?" asked Blaze.

Ha! He'd just enjoyed the best fruit in southern China. It didn't take much convincing to get Blaze to concede that that was enough for one evening.

TOKYO – 2015

Commuter Crisis

In a strange land, blending right in doesn't always help.

"Stop!" shouted Martin.

What, was he crazy? I thought.

For the first time this morning, I'd actually been on point, ahead of Martin and Craig, as we power-walked from the hotel to the subway station. It wasn't yet 8:30am, and I was already feeling my pressed long-sleeved button down starting to paste itself into the small of my back This was July in Tokyo, and it was going to be a steamer.

On the escalator up to the platform, I could hear our train rumbling into the station. I put the spurs on. I needed to get on that train and under the healing blast of the always powerful Tokyo subway car air-conditioners The guys were a bit slow, but I was confident they'd board in time.

Now, with one foot inside the subway car, I paused to look down the track to where Martin was waving frantically at me to join him and Craig. Craig's tall frame ducked into the car and disappeared. Martin waved even more vigorously.

Tokyo subway trains make notoriously short pauses at each station, so I wasn't at all sure I could get the 30 meters down the platform before the doors closed. It was commute hour, and we were lucky to be able to jump into any car.

It made no sense at all, but I could see intensity in his actions. I glanced quickly into the car I would not now be entering. It was nearly full, mostly what the Japanese chauvinistically call Office Ladies (OLs). The car also had a few older, gray-haired women with shopping bags.

I couldn't ignore Martin as he was our local host.

Shoving back from the open door, I accelerated down the platform to where Martin valiantly now stood half inside the train, his arm and head still visible, waving me vigorously onward. It would be close at best.

The chime sounded and the door started closing. I was still a good distance away, but Martin used his body as a human lever. The doors closed on his chest, then quickly re-opened. I leapt inside, panting like an Olympic sprinter, which I most certainly was not and never will be.

"Dude," I tried to say, but gave it up when I saw this car was even less crowded than the one I'd nearly piled into. I grabbed a swinging handhold as the train accelerated out of the station. I scanned until I saw a man reading. His newspaper was rattling in the breeze.

Air-conditioning! I sidled up to him. The cold air was like an anesthetic salve on a third degree burn. I leaned forward and let it blow down the back of my neck. The frigid air hit the sweat on my back, creating a wondrous freezing sensation.

Across from me, Craig had actually found a bench seat. Martin continued to stand by the door we'd come through, now checking his Blackberry.

I sweat like a pig. Dogs don't sweat at all; they release excess heat by panting. I sweat so much that I've tried to pant to reduce the flow, and I've found it does work – a little. If I'm not in a public space and have the gumption, I may pant madly, which is something one ought never do on a well-populated Tokyo subway car. This wasn't my first rodeo doing business in the inferno of a Tokyo summer, where formalwear was still mandated.

I had learned never to put my suit coat on – not while walking, and not while on the subway or in a taxi. My strategy is to wait until the last moment. When we entered the customer's elevator, heading up to their offices, that's when I'd slip on my coat. It helped me minimize the level of drench. The coat would cover the pit stains and the sin of being soaked in one's own body fluids. All this was now second nature.

What made no sense was Martin's frantic act that forced me to sprint onto this particular subway car.

The train smoothly rattled into the twelfth or thirteenth stop. Next one was ours. Martin sidled over to tell me something. He waved at Craig and gestured him over. He wanted to tell us both.

"Next one's ours." To me, he said: "You know what you did wrong, right?"

"I have no idea," I told him. "But I look forward to being enlightened." He was, after all, our native guide, even though he was from Seattle, and, if anything he looked more white than I did.

Nonetheless, he'd lived here 20 years. He and his Japanese wife were raising two teenagers here. He knew what was what.

"Well, I suppose you might have gotten away with it. You're gaijin, after all."

"I resemble that remark," I said flippantly, Three Stooges style.

"Alright, listen up, wise guys," he said to us both, extending the Stooges theme. "Do you know Devin Yamamoto?"

We both did. He was the legendary design engineer in our field, and a fellow employee. "Of course."

"Well, I just don't want a repeat of what happened to Devin. That's all." Then, because our stop was coming up in less than a minute, he quickly told the story.

Devin lived in LA and jokingly called himself "a banana" – yellow on the outside, white on the inside. He had come to Tokyo to do some sales calls just a month ago. He'd stayed for a week, and after a while he insisted that Martin go home and see his family while he explored the Ginza and found his own dinner. Martin finally agreed. It's Tokyo. It's a very safe city And it's hard to get into a whole lot of trouble, unless you're looking for it; then, it's not hard at all. Devin was legendary for being conservative, quiet, and not at all a rabble-rouser.

Which is why what happened to him was even more surprising.

After a hard day of customer visits, Martin had left him at the hotel. Devin had cleaned up and strolled to the subway to catch a train one stop down the line to the heart of the Ginza. He planned to buy some keepsakes for his family from the shops of this notoriously stylish and expensive district of Tokyo.

The train had pulled into the station, and Devin had blithely leapt aboard. It was very crowded, and the crowd was all women. Office ladies, senior ladies, and young ladies in their student uniforms with their Hello Kitty backpacks, dyed-orange hair, and neat black ties.

Most of them were glaring at Devin. He tried to look out the window. It was very uncomfortable. His eyes would drift back to a hardened female face, and he would smile. That didn't help at all.

Then, just seconds into the ride, a gray-haired woman who had been particularly piercing in her glare, stood, walked over to Devin, and began to lambaste him. She let into him something fierce, with shaking finger in his face, essentially snarling. Her voice grew louder. She paused to let him respond, and when he didn't, she really exploded. In Japanese, of course.

Devin didn't speak Japanese. Not one word. But he sure looked Japanese, and therein lay the problem.

Two other older women joined the first. They began to harangue Devin with the same ferocity. He backed against the subway door he'd just come through, hoping it would open soon and let him out.

"I don't know what you're saying!" he bellowed, truly losing his cool. "No comprendo!"

Then, mercifully, the train stopped. The doors opened, and Devin practically fell out of the train and stumbled away. Shouts of rage rose behind him. Then the doors closed, and the subway accelerated out of the station.

A station master with a diagonal black belt over his blue uniform grabbed Devin by the arm. He informed Devin of something very important, and began pulling him toward a little kiosk. It looked to Devin like he was being arrested.

"Stop!" he shouted. "I'm American!" Then he dug into his backpack and pulled out his U.S. passport. The station master paused, considered the document, flipped it open. Then he looked up at Devin and said something in a condescending tone. Nobody knows what it was, but it felt to Devin like "you should be ashamed of yourself." Then he pointed at the painted sign on the subway platform.

It was some kind of instruction. Devin took a picture of it. "Ok," he said. "Sorry." He was released on his own recognizance and he immediately called Martin.

"Dude," said Martin. "You boarded the females only car. Groping is a huge problem on the Japanese transit system."

"Groping!" exclaimed one of the greatest designers in his field. "I'm not a groper!"

"No? Well, that's good. Either way, don't get in the women only car."

We arrived at our station. As the doors opened Martin noted: "I'm sure you'll be more careful in future."

As Curly of the Stooges might say, "Soi-tant-ly!" And indeed I was.

CAHORS REGION, FRANCE – 1995

The Sandwich

Our first day in France we built up a mighty appetite.

This was to be a big trip for us, a pure European holiday, nearly four weeks of the richest regions of France and Italy. Day one was a tightly-scheduled travel day: planes, trains, and automobiles in that order. Our 747 set down at DeGaulle, then we raced to board a TGV high speed train to Bordeaux, then taxied through light coastal rain to a rental car facility. We were seven, and divided into two vehicles, we began convoying our way southeast into the heart of France, Cahors.

Cahors is a region of vast countrysides, rolling hills, vineyards and tiny hilltop villages with many miles between them. The rain pelted harder as we drove. After sunset, it let up completely. The headlights of our vehicles swept a tunnel of illumination into the darkness and our maps indicated we were closing in on our first base of operations, a 15th century farmhouse where we'd reside for the next five nights.

The owner, a farmer, lived in a nearby house.

He'd assured us, "You won't have any problem finding me, since I'll leave my porch light on for you." It was before GPS was commonly available and we were relatively capable navigators with paper maps, odometers, and compass.

"We've got to be within a mile," said Chris, straining into the night from his shotgun position in the lead vehicle, which I drove. We topped a gentle hill and saw a single light in the distance. "I think that's it."

"How the hell can we be certain?" I asked. But sure enough, we were suddenly passing darkened structures. We were in a village, though it was well spread out. Not another structure had a visible light, though some had curtains dimming the illumination beyond.

"The French are dead serious about conserving energy," said Chris. "So that must be our guiding light."

We pulled into a gravel driveway. It was just past 10:00pm. The farmer emerged from his porch, waving. He and Chris exchanged some words of French, and the farmer indicated he would ride with us to our residence. He jumped into the other vehicle. We followed them. It was nearly a half mile away – through deep darkness.

We piled out and the farmer excitedly gave us the tour. He grabbed a little flashlight in the spacious kitchen, which was dominated by an enormous true butcher block wooden island. He gestured for us to follow, upstairs, downstairs. He even showed us the basement. He instructed us on how to use the little oil lamps and lit candles in each room we visited.

"OK? Au revoir!" he said, refusing a lift back to his house. He strolled into the night back the way we'd come.

"This is incredible," said Dawn. "Look at the thickness of the walls." She was right. We stood looking out the second floor kitchen window. The wall had to be three feet thick. "They don't build them like this in California," someone pointed out.

We quietly chatted in the kitchen about our day tomorrow. We would be heading into nearby Cro Magnon country, and planned to visit the 30,000 year old caves of Lascaux. We stood in an ancient farmhouse in a silent, dark place in one of the most remote regions of France that, in addition to its other attractions, was rich with discovery sites documenting the earliest human civilizations and technological advances.

It's believed that this was one of the first places where modern humans encountered so much prolonged cold weather that they were spurred to invent the bone sewing needle 40,000 years ago. This gave humans the ability to snugly tailor the furs they needed to survive the bitter cold; a competitive advantage that may be why they prevailed against their less capable cousins, the Neanderthal.

"Interesting kitchen," I noted. "There's no refrigerator." Seven voices went quiet, reflecting on that.

Somebody's stomach rumbled.

My wife, Shelly, came downstairs with something in her hand. "This is so great!" she said. Then we all heard it. The unfolding of plastic wrap.

"Whatcha got there?" asked Chris.

"My sandwich from the plane. I'm hungry."

"Jesus," said Arthur. "I'm hungry too. Any other food here?" We did a quick check of the cupboards. There wasn't a morsel food to be found; not even enough for a mouse.

Shelly had innocently bitten into her half-eaten sandwich and was chewing, when she noticed that she now had the undivided attention of six hungry people.

"What?" Shelly weighed all of 100 pounds. Looking at my petite wife, it occurred to me that what she held in her hands, though half-eaten on the plane flight ten hours earlier, was still a reasonably large chunk of sandwich. The logic of gastronomy.

Chris was first to verbalize what we were all thinking. "We're hungry," he said. "We want your sandwich."

"Sure, you guys can all have a bite." She was ever generous. But we did our own calculations.

"Is this the only food?"

In short order, the team inventory completed, "That's it, guys. It's Shelly's sandwich and boy, it looks good."

Realization now struck her. "Back off! It's my sandwich."

The ice was broken. Laughter. We were all going to go hungry for the night. "You did say we could have a bite."

"Sure, ok," she said. "Not too big." The sandwich was passed around. You've got to love civilization. That sandwich passed in turn to each of us, and each of us took a single bite. I won't speak to who took the biggest bite. You could hardly blame me anyway. All forensic evidence was of course obliterated in the event, nobody can prove a thing.

True to the valued framework of human cooperation, what was left of that sandwich came back to Shelly. Her eyes were like saucers in the candlelight. "You guys devoured my sandwich!"

Thankfully, she was laughing. I told her: "You better just eat that last bit, honey, the wolves are hungry tonight."

She did. We joked and laughed a few more minutes, then went to bed, stomachs rumbling.

The next day, and for the next 20 days, we ate more great food than we'd ever had in our lives. We'd survived the night of the sandwich and lived to enjoy the feast of our lives.

One long hungry day of travel

Thanks, Sarlat!

For nothing.

We woke early the next morning to glints of sunshine, and of course a profound sense of hunger. Our first full day in France was tightly scheduled, and as there was no food in the farmhouse and nothing of an eating establishment anywhere nearby, we set our sights on a big lunch and piled into the two cars.

We quickly confirmed that this was a remote and isolated region of France. The town of Cro Magnon didn't appear far off; though our reading of the map left out some key factors. The roads were thin, winding through low hills and festooned with hairpin turns. Traffic was minimal, but always very slow. There were a few other tourists, all on a more leisurely agenda than we, but mostly tractors and ultra-wide trucks hauling everything from hay to livestock and some with late-harvest grapes. The land alternated between low, dense forest and rolling hills. Signs of human habitation were few and kilometers between.

The weather was a factor in our slow progress as

well. The sunshine had quickly been chased from the sky by thickening clouds that packed themselves into dark, oppressive storm formations. These began to emit dense squalls of rain; each drop smacked the windshield loudly and the sheet of liquid occluding our vision was hardly swept away by the wipers before forming again. The Mistral made itself felt as well; I drove the lead car, and occasionally felt the wind grip our vehicle and push it toward the edge of the road. I had no choice but to slow.

"The guidebook says this is common for fall," Chris pointed out, sitting shotgun and snapping through the well-worn Rick Steve's guide we'd used to research the trip. "Funny, Dawn never mentioned it."

Dawn, in the other car, was our official tour guide. She'd lived in France for a year, and was best friend of Hailey, Chris's wife. "She can't predict everything," said Hailey. Dawn had stated her determination to craft the itinerary for the two weeks through France to our liking as practice for a possible future career as a tour guide. Chris, ever meticulous, had shadowed some of her research, and already seemed at variance with Dawn's chosen logistics before we'd even boarded the flight to Paris.

"We've got to be getting close to Cro Magnon," I said by way of deflection. "These woods seem positively prehistoric." We'd entered a dense forest that was moist and loamy with moss hugging many of the trunks. The ambient illumination had so diminished, it seemed we were headed into night, yet it wasn't quite 11:00am. We passed a sign, one of the few we'd seen the entire way, that announced: "Pre-Histo Park - 200 meters." The accompanying artwork included a large-browed Cro-Magnon man swinging a wooden club at the open jaws of a saber tooth tiger. The only other sign we'd seen had said "Sarlat: 20km," to which Chris had grumbled: "Hmmm."

"Pre-Histo Park looks great," Chris quipped. "Press on. We'll be lucky to get to Cro Magnon before noon."

We pulled in front of the museum of natural history in the tiny hamlet of Cro Magnon at 11:55. The sun had re-appeared, and steam rose from the shrubs surrounding the medieval walls of the building. All was right with the world as Dawn led us into the museum lobby.

"Merde!" was the first thing I heard, coming in last of the pack. "Merde!" Dawn was clearly upset, her blue eyes flashing at the ticketing attendant.

"Problem?" I asked. Chris was shaking his head.

"Yes, of course there's a problem," he said. "We've arrived right before lunch time. Museum is closing. For two hours. The French are nothing without a long-ass lunch."

The day's schedule was now unravelling. It started to look calamitously worse when it became evident the microscopic village contained no restaurants, and here we had just barely survived the night with a single bite of a half-eaten sandwich each -- and no breakfast.

Dawn looked very unhappy, but her command of French won through. "Where can we have lunch?" she shouted at the attendant, who was very busy trying to close the ticket window on us. "Où pouvons-nous aller déjeuner?"

The attendant wore an expression of extreme

impatience. "There is a store," she said by way of tossing us a bone. "You might buy some kind of food there."

Redemption! And in a big way. The tiny market sold baguettes, gorgeous wedges of brie, and cans of duck liver pâté. We loaded up and included a couple of bottles of red wine, all very reasonably priced, and found a picnic table by a small stream. With the sun and clouds pleasantly exchanging dominance in the topaz blue sky, we used Chris's Swiss Army knife to tear into it. We feasted.

"Dear God," said Arthur. "Dear God, this is good." Dawn, his fiancée, smiled and jammed his mouth with another chunk of baguette loaded down with brie. The rest of us could not have agreed more. After 24 hours of near-starvation, we had begun a period of feasting that was to be unrivaled in our lives. It was a tasty soft-entry to the gluttony that was to come.

When the museum reopened at 2:00pm, we were enthralled. This region of France represented one of the truly great findings in the patchwork story of human civilization. The Cro-Magnon, essentially us, had gained a foothold here against the frozen winters and the imposing physical strength of their adversaries, the Neanderthals, 30,000 years ago. Some 5,000 years after, the Neanderthals were gone, and modern people began to dream, to paint, to carve, and to render their marks which managed to live down the ages, to today.

On the drive back to our farmhouse, which followed a different route leading us to some other human origin sites for which we had little time in the fading sunlight, we again saw a sign for Sarlat.

"Hmmm…" said Chris yet again, digging into yet another guidebook. "Three stars. Three fucking Michelin stars."

We had an incredible week in Cahors. We saw Lascaux, we crawled into the "domes," or ancient stone houses built 10,000 years ago. We ate very, very well. We did, on the other hand, drive an inordinate fraction of each day. And we seemed to pass signs for Sarlat frequently, which taunted Chris no end. "A perfectly representative medieval town," he read, "exceedingly well preserved and a NOT TO BE MISSED attraction when visiting the remote Cahors region of France."

We must have seen everything of interest around Sarlat, except Sarlat itself.

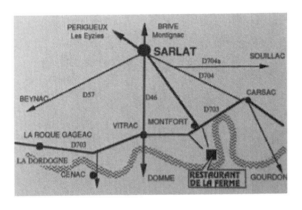

All roads lead to Sarlat. We still never got there.

THE SOUTH OF FRANCE – 1995

A Week In Provence

Not nearly enough by far.

Visiting Provence for a single week is akin to eating one potato chip. The memory, the longing, the lingering flavors can tangle one's thoughts with reflection and distraction.

Provence is a region riddled with hilltop towns, each its own little medieval fortress. There are a few cities, and most of these are not to be missed attractions. The Roman colosseum at Arles rivals its far more famous sibling in Rome for size and is better preserved and more accessible. Avignon, once the seat of the Potentate itself, is loaded with both Roman and more "recent" French historic relics, architecture, and art. We enjoyed all these sights.

But mostly, we ate. And we enjoyed that even more.

Before Provence, I'd never sat still for a three hour lunch. Ever after, I dream of doing it again, in the warm open sunshine, under a sky so fiercely blue it doesn't seem real, at a café with only three tables and nearly full focus by the chef on our needs. Being in yet another hillside town, the café afforded us sweeping vistas of the rolling Provençal countryside. Vats of wild boar stew, venison cutlet, delicately fileted breast of quail, all manner of mushrooms and an onion soup hidden by an impenetrable dome of melted cheese, were just a few of the chef's specialties.

The waitstaff was the chef's daughter, in her young twenties, and an able server with the flair expected from the French, but with attentiveness nothing like we'd experienced in this country of infamously perturbed and distracted waiters. Her long, red hair was in a single thick ponytail that reached her waist, and occasionally was felt gently on our backs as she whirled to attend to our gustatory needs.

The greatest servers often say nothing. I've never been a server (except for the few sorry hours I spent taking orders at a McDonalds counter, before the manager realized his error and sent me back to the grill), so my opinion shouldn't count, but here it is: great servers don't ask if you need….anything. They just bring it, and make sure there's more before you think more is even needed. She asked only one thing: "Where do you go next?" and that after espresso and just before we gathered the fortitude to stand and start asking each other the same question.

"What do you recommend?" asked Dawn in French.

"You must proceed to the chapel at 4pm," she explained. "You may have a chance to ring the town bells."

It turned out, no, the friars had decided the bells

needed oiling. Clambering up the bell tower to see that process gave us an extra 25 meters of altitude; not much, except when added to the height of the town, enough though that looking out felt like walking with the gods. The vista was breathtaking.

That was it for this tiny town. We drove a few kilometers to a much larger venue, Forcalquier. Even in the late day, it was swarming with shoppers and tourists, plying the cheese shops, the prosciutto shops, the shops that sold things that might or might not have come from frogs.

A street musician played his mandolin with passion, bellowing out a French shanty that I wished I could find. When he finished with a flourish, he drew a deep breath and began the exact same song again. And again. It was as if this was the town's own special song. I couldn't get it out of my head. It was good, but it became an ear worm. Many years later I tried to hum it into a song recognition app, but I don't hum any better than I whistle, so no luck. Nevertheless, that song is still stuck there, directly between my ears. It probably will be there forever, or at least until the onset of Alzheimer's.

The light was draining from the sky when we returned to our village and our farmhouse. This one was even grander than the one in Cahors. Here, the mademoiselle lived under the same roof, and she cooked. Dinner came every night if requested in advance, and most of that week we did request.

We sat at a large table set with a white linen tablecloth, and dishes began to emerge from the kitchen shortly thereafter, nearly 9:00pm. With the first dish came a lacquered pitcher containing perhaps three liters of red wine. It was the house wine, evidently refilled from a secret hose under the table.

"Oui," she said, responding to someone's query. "I make it." Aside from mineral water and espresso, it was the only liquid she served that week. It made everything taste great.

Even frog legs. Even escargot. And most especially, the putrefied stinky near liquid cheeses that made some unhappy, but sent Chris and me into an altered state of gourmand heaven. It had to be spooned out of a vat onto the chunks of baguette, and it reeked in a wondrous way.

If you don't care much for cheese, or have lactose intolerance, you might not appreciate the magnitude of impact on my psyche that this gloriously foul cheesy comestible imparted. Think of the smell of Limburger, and the taste of raw grass, the kind you ate briefly as a kid when the baseball game went badly for your face. Think of pungency and odiferousness on an almost nuclear scale. There was butter, there was essence of cow, and there was a feral animality about every dripping, chewy bite.

God, that was a cheese to remember.

In the event it wasn't your thing, the vats of duck liver pâté always followed. Please, vegetarians, vegans, and those for whom your omnivore origins are less celebrated – please, please remember how hard our species has struggled lo these 500 million years in order to stand atop the food chain. Can we not all, ever so briefly on the timescale of this universe, pause to enjoy our pole position? Not long ago, we were the hunted, and in the future, well, who knows. The giant silver spiders might employ *us* as their incubators, with our still wriggling web-entrapped bodies serving as fresh sustenance for their fledglings. My food recommendation: relax, and enjoy a little pâté now and then.

This particular pâté was creamy, rich salve that rolled back the bare-naked bovine-ness of the liquid cheese. It opened new dimensions of flavor sensation, equally primitive, but in its own way, more civilized. Ducks are, after all, among the most successful of the dinosaurs – avians that survived the Earth's run-in with that asteroid 65 million years ago, and went on to develop not just flight, but the ability to swim. Very few species have command of land, sea, and air; and the few others that can claim these achievements don't taste nearly as delectable.

The seven of us always toasted the duck pâté. It was an extravaganza of sensation that had to be recognized. We honored the ducks their sacrifice. It was, in truth, the very least we could do for them, after their little livers had done so much for us. All hale the duck!

With the pâté feast complete, dinner came on. There were platefuls of smoking hot delicacies doused in the most incredible sauces. We took turns each night being the first to have a faux heart attack. All in good fun, and a way to communicate that the end was near and sleep would shortly be our next best move.

In the morning we woke to a brilliant blue sky, skipped breakfast, and did it all again. Just like you're supposed to. That was our week in Provence. Gluttony on a scale that should be illegal in every decent nation on Earth.

Viva la France!

When Worlds Collide

Hollywood and Silicon Valley are a tough mix.

"Robert who?"

"Evers," said Jeff, though that wasn't exactly his real name. "He's a top-dog at Pyramid Studios, and he wants to meet with us." Jeff was one hell of a salesman, but I just didn't get it. "He's close friends with Dustin Hoffman," he added, as if that would make it all click for me.

We were developing an electronic point-of-sale system for the home. The system would allow anyone anywhere anytime to swipe their credit card from the comfort and safety of their living room sofa, while say watching Home Shopping Network. Badda bing badda boom! You just bought merchandise while eating popcorn. Today we call this eCommerce and much of it happens on Amazon, but at the time, it was an exciting and novel proposition.

"Ok, when do we want meet this Evers guy?"

"He's asked us to come by his office Thursday."

It was a tremendous oak paneled space, in a building near the center of the Pyramid Studios lot, with multiple comfy chairs and sofas and one immense leather chair. Evers stood as we were escorted to him as did three other people. One was introduced as "my lawyer, Stanton," another was his chief of staff. The third, dressed like a starlet, a blond-haired beauty was not introduced. That didn't slow Jeff down.

"Hi," he rushed at her and offered his hand as she giggled.

"That's Tina," said Stanton. "My girlfriend." That's Hollywood.

Evers was very animated and excited. After we'd been seated, he stood and began pacing while he spoke. "You know, this has been a very exciting career here in cinema. Now I sense it's time to expand, to explore new frontiers of business and entertainment. That's why I love your…what do you call it again?"

"Domestic Point of Sale System," said Jeff. "It's going to revolutionize commerce and finance."

Evers was digging it. "Exactly! Yes, that's what it is. Now, we need to get started immediately. I'll be right back." He suddenly strolled out of the room.

Thirty minutes later, his assistant stood and apologized. "Folks, sorry for the delay, let me go see what's keeping Robert."

It turned out Robert had suddenly gone to Santa Barbara for the weekend. "I'm dreadfully sorry. He called me from the car and asked if you could come to the house on Monday."

"Robert's house?"

"Yes, it's quite close by in the Hills." Beverly, that is.

The house was fabulous and leafy, with huge

mature trees making it a sanctum. It was loaded with movie memorabilia. We waited in the living room for a few minutes.

"Now," said Evers, walking in wearing the cliched bathrobe one expects eccentric Hollywood moguls to wear around their house, "Where were we?"

Evers was quickly back in the groove. "Yes, I have a strong, clear vision now. I can see it, Jeff. This new…what's it called Home thing…it's going to make our lives wonderful. Now, here's what we need. We need someone to write a letter to my boss."

"Your boss?" said Jeff

"His boss is Summer Bluerock," said Stanton. "He owns Pyramid and a lot of other stuff."

"Yes, yes," said Robert. "Summer will be very impressed with this device."

"Tim here can write the letter," MY boss, Jeff, volunteered.

"Sure," I said. "Happy to."

"That's excellent, absolutely splendid," said Evers, turning to me probably for the first time in our two meetings. "Now, how is this device going to transport us into the 21ˢᵗ century?" He seemed sincerely interested in my answer.

"To be honest, Robert, we're going directly into the 21ˢᵗ century with or without our device." He looked into my eyes expectantly, so I thought it best to add something more to this observation.

"We'll just all be able to cope with it better if we have the Domestic Point of Sale system."

"Yes!" he pointed a finger at the ceiling. "Exactly! You will write the letter. That's exactly the kind of brand messaging Summer is certain to respond to."

I returned home from Hollywood and wrote a two-page letter. It was a very impressive treatise, at least, that's what Evers told me when he reviewed it over the phone. "Brilliant! You should come work in Hollywood."

Evers forwarded the letter to his immensely powerful boss. Jeff followed up a week later, and Stanton told us that Summer had not yet responded. As far as I know he never did. We went on to sell our device to other, more application focused organizations. Sure enough, we did enter the 21st century, but that was the start, middle, and end of my Hollywood career. Almost.

LONDON – 2018

Blocked by Giants

The great cathedrals are destinations of pilgrimage, and the realm of giants.

We woke early our first morning in London, skipped breakfast, tidied ourselves, and kitted up for tourism: cameras, fanny packs, shorts, t-shirts, sneakers. Cash and coins for the Tube and "comfort breaks," a common term used by Brits for a quick nose-powdering. When given a very short stay in one of the most vast and historically rich cities in the world, agility is mandatory. We were on schedule for a big day of sightseeing in the wonderfully diverse seat of the British Empire.

Failing to make complete sense of the famous Underground map, (an exact copy of the scar on Albus Dumbledore's left knee, I understand it) I checked with the concierge.

"Westminster Abby is it then? Brilliant," the middle-aged man in uniform informed us. "Just pop-on over to Blackfriar station, take the District line west and alight at Westminster. Single jump, no worries." I meticulously read back to him what I scribbled as he spoke, just to be sure. "Right you are,

Bob's your uncle." That sounded good.

It was. We emerged into the sunshine at Westminster and faced Big Ben and Parliament to our left, and the great cathedral straight ahead.

We approached the entrance, anticipating a stroll through its majesty atop the smooth-worn marker stones of hundreds of the world's leading luminaries to history – Charles Darwin, Sir Isaac Newton, Charles Dickens, and Queen Elizabeth I among them. It soon became clear that something was off.

The growing crowd ahead of us was dressed to kill. Ladies wore fancy hats and fashionable dresses. Men were in formal suits and ties and some even sported top hats. There were men and women in military dress, complete with gleaming medals and a variety of uniforms from a multitude of nations.

My wife, Shelly, raced ahead to ask an authoritative young lady who stood on the Abby side of the wrought-iron barrier that screened the immaculately dressed crowd from entering. She asked "what time does the Abby open?"

"Oh, so sorry," the lady responded. "The Abby will be closed today. It's a special commemoration for Stephen Hawking."

My daughter, Michelle, perked up at that. "Is Neil DeGrasse Tyson coming?"

"How about Bill Nye the Science Guy?" I added.

She laughed. "I really don't know. It depends on the Hawking family invitation list." Clearly there were many on that list, and the service wouldn't even begin for another 90 minutes.

It was amazing. Hawking was the most famous physicist since Einstein, and had held the same academic seat of honor at Oxford as Sir Isaac

Newton, and we had bumbled into his ceremony. It was a déjà vu experience from 20 years prior.

Back then, Shelly and I had reached Notre Dame de Paris mid-day, and a giant crowd, also well dressed, was streaming out. It turned out to be the life service of France's greatest undersea explorer, and one of the most influential environmentalists of the 20th century. I'd watched his television series as a kid with rapt attention, but to me he was most notable as the inventor of the aqualung and modern scuba-diving -- Jacques Yves Cousteau.

As chance had it, the French authorities were quick to usher us tourists into the mighty cathedral afterward so we did see Notre Dame that day.

Not so with Westminster Abby. It would remain closed until at least late in the day, and we wouldn't be able to circle back with our tight itinerary.

Sure, we were bummed about not getting into Westminster. But we spent 30 minutes chatting with some of the soldiers, scientists, friends and family of the Hawkings. It was a magic moment on this trip. We'd tried to see the house of the greats, and had been blocked by a giant of science.

A fair exchange. No complaints.

UNITED KINGDOM – 2018

Customer Service

Serve the Customer, not "The System."

Our London hotel was right next to the magnificent dome of St. Paul's Cathedral, which made leaving early even tougher. Now this!

"Sir," said the hotel manager, a middle-aged woman in a finely pressed uniform jacket, "you're free to leave the hotel one day early, but I can't give you any refund. The system makes that impossible."

"Impossible?" I asked, more politely than I felt was merited. "Are you sure? You're over-booked for tonight."

"It's not our fault you have to leave early," she responded. "It's a non-refundable rate you have."

"Yes," I agreed, "I'm making the decision to leave one night early." I'd already explained to her why, which seemed to have been a matter of extreme indifference for her. I had to be in Brussels on Monday morning for business; no excuses. Traveling with my family who was on European holiday while I did my business – permitting me to enjoy occasional sightseeing and meals with them -- meant it would be most inconvenient if they, too, weren't in Brussels on Monday as well.

Thus, I'd booked us all tickets on the Chunnel (Channel Tunnel) train weeks in advance for Sunday. Now, just two days before our journey, the French Rail Network announced a nationwide strike for Sunday and Monday. We'd have to pivot. We decided to travel to the continent one day early, just ahead of the looming strike. Changing train tickets and rental cars had been easily arranged.

Past experience with hundreds of hotel check-ins and many dozens of improvised schedules informed me that if the hotel was slow the night we were vacating, and we had already pre-paid at a discounted fare, a refund would be a hard sell. Even so, most times it was achievable with the right attitude and explanation.

In all prior cases such as this, where the hotel was sold out and customers were being turned away, it had always been a slam dunk. "What? What's that you say?" the desk manager would ask, just to be sure he wasn't being played, trying to hold back a happy grin. "You have to check out one day early? Oh, I say, let me see what can be done." It was his chance to be a hero to a customer on the waitlist or to one of the many walk-ins he would otherwise have to disappoint face-to-face. He would then charge the new customer a large premium over what he was refunding me, and thus be a hero to at least two customers while pocketing extra profits for the hotel. Win-win-win.

I tried to outline this happy scenario to the manager. "Look, Megan," I said, calling her Megan as that was what her name tag read. "I'm terribly sorry to trouble you, but you'd be doing one customer – me – a huge favor, and you'd be ready to warmly welcome the next harried traveler who comes through that door," I pointed at the revolving glass door of the hotel for effect. "You would make two customers happy while collecting more revenue for your hotel; thus making your boss happy as well."

"Terribly sorry, sir, the system simply won't allow me to re-market your room. It's already been sold, and you bought it. That's it."

Hmm. A line of guests and check-ins was forming behind me. I made myself comfortable, put my elbow on the counter, and rested cheek on palm. "So, just to be perfectly clear," I said. Megan nodded quickly, her eyes darting over my shoulder at the gathering crowd behind me.

"If I abandon my room, but change my mind and come back at say, midnight, my key will open the door, and I'll be able to flop onto the bed and get a fit snooze."

"That's right, sir," she said enthusiastically.

"Even if twelve people come through here demanding a room," I drilled further, "You'll tell them we're sold out, no rooms available, even though my room IS available?"

"Have to, sir," she said. "No choice. It's controlled by the system."

"Does this system have a boss?"

"Yes, here is her card." I looked at it closely. It had an email address and a phone number, but no name.

"Her? Does she have a name?"

"Oh, yes," said Megan, "let me write it down for you." She scrawled, 'Madeline.'

"OK, Megan," I relented, "my booking agent will call you shortly, and meantime I'll talk to Madeline. I appreciate your candor. Having said that, you do see why this system of yours makes no sense?"

"Sir, it's non-refundable," she reminded me, quite needlessly.

"You keep saying that, Megan, but refunds are granted by humans. They're business decisions, and you're telling me it's impossible for your hotel to make a good business decision in this situation."

I knew I was at the extreme limit of her patience, so I turned to the elevator.

Madeline never answered my phone call. Within minutes, however, Megan did indeed get a call from my booking agent. Afterwards, the agent called me back. "I'm so sorry, Mr. Jenkins. This situation makes no sense to us either. We can't force the hotel to do the right thing, but we can give you $250 credit."

"That would be wonderful," I told her. I'd booked hundreds of rooms with these guys. I was a valued customer. At least, I certainly felt like one.

A few minutes later, I gave Megan a handwritten note addressed to her boss, congratulating her on the professional and courteous nature of her staff and the excellent quality of the hotel. I also admonished that her "system" was working against the hotel's success, and offered to talk with her at any time of her convenience on this topic.

Megan was ecstatic to receive a letter of praise instead the nasty complaint she'd expected. Then the coup de grace came as my wife gave her a leftover bottle of spirits we didn't want to haul on the train to France.

"You're so kind!"

"Feel free to have a hotel staff party in our room tonight and drink it!!" Everybody laughed.

Win. Win. Win.

PARIS – 2016

How to Negotiate With a Street Vendor

Haggle like it's real money.

Knowing how to negotiate is important, especially when you travel. During my first trip to China, I still had no idea how to buy things. Yes, sure, I knew everything was negotiable and a tussle was expected. Haggling is standard protocol in most street markets the world over.

The first conversation I had on the Great Wall went something like this: "How much is this?"

"Twenty RMB," said the tanned, youthful vendor. That was not the price. That was the starting point. She and her sister or cousin or counterpart were doing a very good business. I waited patiently for the opportunity to look closely at the wares. They were actually very nice shirts, thick white cotton with an excellent red imprint of the Great Wall stretching off, winding over the hills into the distance, with the words "Great Wall of China Shirt" smartly laid out beneath.

What more could you want? I needed this shirt. "No, twenty is too much," I countered. "Fifteen."

"OK," she said, "here you go!"

What had I done? I had my shirt for less than $3, but somehow I felt like a total sucker.

That experience taught me a valuable lesson that would save me many thousands of dollars in the future. Since you never know where the real floor is, when you haggle, the general rule of thumb is to start just as low as physically possible. It's a worthwhile process and, importantly, it satisfies both buyer and seller.

By way of illustration, flash forward many years, to my family and friends on vacation in Paris. It was a beautiful sunny day at a large hilltop park overlooking the Eiffel Tower. It was our second day in Europe and I'd been snapping photos in an awkward manner with my brand new and expensive smartphone. With each pic I risked the phone slipping out of my fingers or being jostled by the crowds of Parisian tourists. We spied a vendor selling selfie sticks. It occurred to me, one of those would be incredibly handy.

My daughter and I walked up to the vendor.

"How much?"

He held up the selfie stick, smiled, and telescoped it; he angled it back and forth. He waved it. "Twenty Euro," he said. A piece of plastic and a cheap metal tube. I remembered my lesson at the Great Wall and I dug deep.

"One Euro," I offered.

My thirteen-year-old daughter almost hit me. "Dad, don't insult him!"

She did have something there. The first time I bid on a house, my realtor "tsked-tsked" when I said my bid would be 85% of asking. "If you bid less than

90% of asking, you risk offending the seller." That was perfectly fine by me. I offended that seller and two or three more. Ultimately, I became a homeowner without overpaying.

But the selfie-stick man just smiled. Eighteen he said. I repeated my bid.

"Fifteen!" he said.

"One point five," I responded. Then I held my ground until he got to 5 Euros. I went to 2 Euros.

"Four!"

I turned to walk away, and my kid gets full credit for doing the same. We were almost out of earshot when the vendor yelled, "OK! Two Euros!" We strolled back. "I lose money, but you're nice."

That selfie-stick went on to annoy a great many fellow tourists at the Mona Lisa, Eiffel Tower, and a wide swath of France's most treasured sights. The photos were nice keepsakes, and all for less than the shirt had cost me at the Great Wall long before. It no doubt saved me from dropping my fancy phone a few times as well.

Proof of the achievement was my teenage daughter actually praising me. "Great job on the selfie-stick, dad!"

Now that's how haggling is done.

Assassination

"There is no greater thrill than to be shot at without result."
-- Winston Churchill

Churchill made this reflection in a book he wrote about his experiences in The Boer War. I could see what he meant, until the day I realized that there was one greater thrill: being shot at **with** result but suffering no permanent long term effects; except to the ego.

My friends and I were already maximizing play on the primitive computer and video games available at the time – Laser Skeet on the PC, Asteroids and Rip-Off at the arcade – and we still had plenty of adrenaline left over. Normal kids would be improving their lay-up or kicking a three-pointer from the forty yard line. Not us. We had much more exciting pursuits vying for our free time.

There was chess, of course. A fallback grudge match could be arranged almost anywhere on short notice. There were board games such as Risk and Monopoly that could pass the time on a Sunday afternoon, but far better were the day-long marathons with octagonal-based military strategy board games such as World War II, Stalingrad, and Blitzkrieg. The space based board games were OK, too, but lost something for having to be reduced to the meager two dimensions of the board.

These were great distractions from the pressures of college. They were pleasant, social affairs, spiced by vast quantities of chips, nuts, and sugary sodas. They paled, however, in comparison to the live-action games: the rubber-tipped dart gun wars, mass population team hide-and-seeks that began after midnight, and the occasional capture the flag championships. In an age when paintball and laser tag were just around the corner, we'd perfected games that, in some ways, were even more thrilling.

The greatest of all was Assassination. The objective was self-explanatory. One thrill of the game was in the mystery of who had been assigned to assassinate whom. Governed by a single organizer (often referred to as "M") who also served as officiator, dozens of players often participated. There were no teams, it was total elimination until one lone Assassin survived and was crowned victor. Although behavior was strictly constrained by the honor system, there were never any holds barred; death could be visited on any player, anytime, in any form.

It was intense. It was exhilarating. Adding to the thrill was the fact that there was no time limit, and the game might play out for many days, a week, even longer. Most thrilling of all: it was played out in full view of the world, friends, family, schoolmates and teachers. In this regard, it was no different from a James Bond or Jason Bourne movie, in which each player was compelled to move through the course of their normal activities and blend in with the rest of society, while hunting their quarry to extinction; and while being themselves hunted by a familiar, but unknown, enemy.

It was kill, then kill again, and keep killing, until you yourself were killed, or declared the victor. As victims were eliminated, they would dutifully hand over the name of their next target to their assassin. With each "death" the circle tightened and the circumstances became grimmer for those left alive.

In one of the largest mass games I was ever in, we received our secret targets on Friday and the action officially began Sunday at midnight the week before midterm exams. Most of the players, though not all, were students at Cal State University Long Beach. My victim was Paul, a fellow student I would take down on Tuesday afternoon. It was when we had a geology lab together, and I had devised a nasty trap there for Paul. My plan was to wait until we were at the lab bench together.

I would drop the boom on poor Paul, and he would never see it coming. We had a lab manual that we used frequently. Once we were in the swing of things, I would ask Paul to open the manual to page 55, where we both knew there was helpful reference data. There, I had inserted one of those annoying new greeting cards with a tiny battery and sound chip. As the card sang "happy birthday" I would inform Paul that he had just breathed in nerve gas, and was now dead. He would then smile, perhaps oblige with a dramatic gagging scene, and give me the name of the person who would become my next victim.

All day Monday, as I sprinted from class to class, I kept the eyes in the back of my head very busy indeed. Friends greeted each other warily, with big smiles, and all of us kept a little extra distance from each other. No attempts were made on my life, to my knowledge. College is a busy time and the week before midterms is busier than most. It was easy to get distracted by the task at hand, but I kept my eagle-like attention to where I was, who else was nearby, and what possible means they might use to inflict upon me an untimely demise.

I made it through Monday unscathed, and was looking forward to taking down my first victim and moving on the next quickly thereafter. As Calculus wrapped up, Rob and I – who were pretty sure neither of us was now the target of the other – decided to walk over to grab a bite at the campus's big open air eatery. Rob had brought his lunch in a brown paper bag, and I bought a burger.

We sat across from each other at a picnic table deep inside the crowded space of the eating area, uncomfortably aware of how exposed we were. I was keeping a sharp eye out for Rob – I had his back, you might say – and he did the same for me. Occasionally he would straighten up. Rob is a tall guy, even when seated, and he did this in reaction to someone familiar passing not far behind me. His posture mimicked that of a prairie dog popping up to spy approaching danger.

I suppose I was doing something similar. "What's wrong?" Rob asked as my eyes focused on the approaching familiar face of our friend Harry, coming up behind Rob.

Harry wasn't stupid, and he paused a few steps behind Rob to announce himself. "Greetings, gentle-beings," he said, waving his open left hand. In his right was a tray that contained a yogurt and an orange juice bottle. "Might I join you?"

Harry was a good friend from high school, and was an avid science fiction fan and gamer. All three of us were playing Assassin. It was simply a question of who was assigned to kill whom, and how were they planning to do it. Rob shrugged his shoulders. "OK by me," he said, apparently resigned to taking his chances.

"Sure, just keep that backpack on your shoulders," I admonished. I knew it was a risk, but we were almost done eating. Harry clambered onto the bench next to Rob, as Rob removed the last of his lunch, an apple, from the brown bag.

Harry put his tray down. "Great weather," he said. Then I saw the black Sharpee, already open on his lunch tray. I started to get up. Too late.

Harry picked up the Sharpee, reached across the table and swiped a black line on my left hand. "You're dead, Mr. Jenkins," he said. "Contact poison."

Ah, crap. We all had a good laugh.

"Dude," I said, "with a Sharpee? Shit, you don't take any prisoners, do you, Harry?"

"Never," he said.

"Me neither," said Rob, who had crumpled one end of his brown paper bag. He held it up to Harry's head and slapped it with his other hand. It popped loudly.

"Oww!" said Harry, rubbing his ear.

"You're dead too," said Rob. "Directional explosive with ball-bearings."

It was a rare double-killing. We all enjoyed the moment, then Rob realized he needed some key information.

"Paul," I told him. Rob stood immediately.

"Gentlemen," he said by way of excusing himself. "Oh, can I borrow this?" Harry waved in the affirmative, and Rob walked away. With the Sharpee. Harry and I, now freed from the anxiety of trying to stay alive, relaxed a few minutes longer at the table. We speculated on who else might already be dead, and how long this game might play out.

"I heard it's going a lot faster than expected," he said. "There are at least two players with triple kills already." That was extraordinary, so early on. We must have some real terminators in this fracas.

Within ten minutes, a hand fell on my shoulder. "Bad news, guys," said Rob. "Paul is dead." We were all ferocious Beatles fans. That was pretty funny.

The next morning, I caught up with Rob in Astronomy. "I'm dead," he informed me.

"Oh, crap. Sorry about that. What happened?"

Rob had made it through Tuesday. He'd gone to work that night at his guard job, returned home at midnight, and approached the front door with caution. He used his flashlight to check for trip wires and booby-traps. He made it inside the house and slept soundly.

This morning, he was running a little late. It was cold, and his Nissan 210 had some frost on the windshield. He circled the car warily, opened the trunk and got out the Windex and some paper towels. Once cleared up, he was about to open the car door, but decided crouch down and look underneath first.

Sure enough, he found it. A booby trap. Half an aluminum diet coke can secured with a bit of tape to the chassis, with fishing line connecting it to the door.

If he had opened the door, he would have been killed instantly as the can banged on the driveway. As it was, he had found and defused the bomb. Inside the can was a folded note. "If killed, call George." Ha! Now he could stay away from George and maybe win the game.

Relieved, but even more behind schedule, he jumped in and warmed the engine, backed out of the drive, and sped toward school.

"Immediately, I knew I was dead." As he'd put the car in drive and punched it, he heard rattling from behind. He parked at the curb and saw the other half of the coke can was dragging behind him on a long piece of fishing line. A double booby trap. Rob's car had been blown up by the second "bomb."

The game was finished later that day. George was good. He killed the final few players in the afternoon, one after the other, using a variety of furtive methods. For the final victim, he abandoned secretive protocols completely, and whipped out a bright orange dart pistol to shoot Anna – in the back, in class, and in front of the teacher and 40 other students, no less.

"Hey," he later told us all at a celebratory get-together. "It's Assassination. Got to do your job; no mercy."

"I don't blame him a bit," said Anna. "If I'd seen him coming, he'd have been dead instead of me."

Ah, those were the days. The thrill of the chase, the terror of being hunted. The joy of being able to do it again. Now that's gaming!

CAPE CANAVERAL, FLORIDA – 1981

Defending the Press

Excessive force in the defense of a free press is no vice.

At T-minus 18 minutes -- 18 minutes after a decade of anticipation -- the clock stopped. Space shuttle Columbia stood idle, gently out-gassing from its full fuel tanks. History on pause.

"Well, we got a hold," said the flight controller. The 5,000 reporters and photographers assembled at the edge of the Canaveral lagoon seemed to let out a deep sigh, and sure enough the whole launch was scrubbed within the hour. The announcement came: "Well, next launch window is in 47 hours. There'll be a brief press conference at 10am." At the conference, it was revealed that one of the Shuttle Orbiter's five identical and redundant computers was not in sync with the others.

"Why can't you fly with four good computers?" asked one of the press via a microphone.

"We have a perfectly good launch window on Sunday morning," said the flight director over a loud PA system. "We'd rather take a hard look at this issue to understand it." It made sense. Patience and caution are always merited before the maiden flight of an entirely new space transport system. Shortly, the conference broke up, and reporters packed up their cameras, went to their cars, helicopters, press vans with huge antennas on top, and very quickly disappeared from the cape.

NASA had given Jake and I a permit that allowed us to pitch a tent on the edge of the lagoon just three-and-a-half miles from the launch site, which is what we had done the night before. Of course, the place had been thronged then. Those thousands of reporters were there with us, most of them staying up all night. There was excitement in the air. We barely slept ourselves, but today was shaping up differently. Forty-seven hours is two days. By noon, the Cape had been cleared out and we were completely alone. "Well," said Jake, we may as well go into town, be tourists for a while." So we drove to nearby Titusville.

There isn't a lot in Titusville, but we did it justice. We hit some shops. I tried to rent a telephoto lens that the shop owner only wanted to sell, and for a sum far in excess of the total cash we'd brought on the trip. Then we had dinner and came back through the security zone at the Cape as the sun set over the ocean. After strolling along the lagoon in the deepening dusk, and admiring the leap of dolphins and seeing a few paddling alligators, we decided it was time to crawl back into our pup tent.

We zipped the mosquito netting, then began methodically eliminating the half dozen or so flying invaders trapped inside with us. Only one other person was visible anywhere around and that one wore camouflage and a green beret. When it was truly dark, we heard him clomping up toward our tent. He carried an M-16, finger relaxed over the trigger-guard, barrel pointed at the ground.

"Y'all staying overnight here, huh?" he asked with what might have been an Arkansas accent.

"Yup," said Jake.

"Okay. Well I got your back." He laughed.

"Thanks, buddy," said Jake, who himself was in the process of signing up with the US Army. A few short months after this trip, he would ship out to Basic Training.

"Yeah, I mean," said the soldier, "I seriously got your back. My relief comes at 02:00 and I'll brief him, so he'll have your back, too."

That made me feel extra safe in our tent, but I couldn't understand why the worry. The whole cape was under serious lockdown.

"Still," he continued, "Y'all be careful."

"Sure, OK," I said. "What's the worry?"

"Well, I mean, you're probably fine inside the tent. But if you have to get up to take a wiz, do it real careful like. Those gators will be sleeping all around here. If you trip over one, it's apt to take a snap atcha."

That was a bit sobering. We asked the guard to stick around a few minutes while we jogged over to the lagoon in the fading light to void our bladders. By 03:00, I woke again with a pressing need, but decided to tough it out and went back to sleep.

No point tempting fate so close to launch.

PACIFIC NORTHWEST – 1981

Under the Knife

Our road trip to Canada went off the rails.

"Count backward from ten," said the anesthesiologist. Before I did, I asked myself, "how the hell did this happen?"

The Pacific Northwest is the vast, timbered stuff of dreams. Native Americans who came here erected great totem poles of carved faces with expressions seemingly from another dimension. It's the legendary home of Sasquatch, the big-footed near-human still believed by many to haunt the trackless forests of Oregon, Washington, and British Columbia. Somewhere in its vastness, D.B. Cooper and his ransom cash landed after his leap from a jetliner, and no definitive trace of him has ever been confirmed.

Rob and I had sped north on Interstate 5, spent a few hours admiring Crater Lake, and then continued north to stay with his relatives. First, we overnighted with his grandfather, whose place was perched above the mighty Columbia River, not far from Portland. I learned something very useful from him.

"In the winter, it's cold enough that I'll step out

of the shower and use the blow dryer instead of a towel." Now that's travel wisdom worthy of the journey, and just one of many tidbits I garnered on this trip. We stayed the following night at Rob's cousin's place in Kent, Washington. That evening we all went to a drive-in to watch the movie "Stripes" starring Bill Murray. This was early June, 1981, and there were still such diversions to be had.

The road called us back the next morning. We continued our northward charge through Seattle, and then across the Canadian border. It's not much of a foreign nation for Americans – that is to say, it's a wonderful place, with nice people – yet its similarities to America grossly outweigh its differences. Nonetheless, we did our level best, noting that the gas station attendant who filled our empty tank outside Vancouver happily allowed us to pay in U.S. dollars – with a 20% exchange rate incentive for him.

We found a bank and exchanged for Canadian dollars before driving onto a ferry westbound for Victoria. The voyage across the sound in the fading northern light was mystical. Was that a killer whale 300 meters off the starboard bow? Rob assured me it was an otter. Dusk fell upon the sea and we chopped through it toward the forested realm of Vancouver Island. The ride sparked my desire to cruise the Inside Passage to Alaska one day, which I did, 23 years later.

Darkness was still peeling back the daylight slowly as we disembarked in the little town. We enjoyed a quick meal of barbequed pork sandwiches and fries. Then, mustering the faint visibility not mopped up by the filtering giant trees, we drove a few miles further north, to the site of our lodging, which tonight would be a campground. With the aid of my Boy Scout flashlight, we pitched the pup tent, crawled inside, and quickly passed into the actual realm of dreams...

...to awaken a few hours later, to the staccato symphony of a Northwest summer rain pounding the canvas. I guess we both were too wiped to worry about it. I fell back to sleep, and awoke only when chilled to the bone. Our tent had been compromised by nature. Rob and I scrambled out of the sopping sleeping bags and reluctantly piled into his Nissan 210. I shivered in the back while Rob splayed out in the reclined passenger seat. The shivers continued for a long time.

At some point, before a ghostly dawn began to outline the giant trees surrounding us, I felt the pain again. It was the familiar ache in my lower right abdomen, and it quickly grew to a new level I hadn't before experienced. Exhaustion and pain battled, the result was not so much restlessness as writhing punctuated by a series of faints.

In the dawn light, just moving around to build a fire and tramping over to the campground's laundry facility to try to dry some of our clothes somehow mitigated the ache. At least it allowed me to focus on something else.

We breakfasted on stacks of pancakes and fried eggs with actual Canadian bacon at a little coffee shop in Nanaimo. I remember sucking down four or five cups of coffee; more than enough to annoy Rob, who always grew weary of my protracted caffeine binges -- a habit proudly inherited from my father, I suppose.

We had reached the zenith of our northward voyage, and rolled the Nissan onto a ferry by midmorning to return to Vancouver. We drove off the ferry and headed directly south, back toward the U.S.A., toward Long Beach, California. We'd planned for one more Motel 6 stay between here and home, somewhere across the border of our home state.

Not long after crossing Customs and re-entering the U.S., I directed Rob to pull over. The pain in my abdomen was momentarily eclipsed by nausea, and with little discomfort my breakfast retraced its route. Afterward, I felt much better. We drove on.

In the distance as afternoon waned, we observed the collapsed remnants of Mount St. Helens, which one year previously had exploded in volcanic fury, killing more than sixty people who'd ignored evacuation warnings from the U.S. Geological Service. The mighty mountain had been reduced to a shell by its own fury.

We again crossed the Columbia River and were back in Oregon. Another few hours, and we could stop for the night. But it was not to be.

"This town might be good," I suggested to Rob, as we passed a sign that said "Roseburg City Limit." He didn't argue, and we quickly found the Motel 6 and checked in. My gut was throbbing. Since breakfast, I'd barely been able to nibble a granola bar and sip a few drops of water. A good night's sleep in a dry bed, I felt sure, would put things right.

I lay on the bed while Rob fetched some dinner for us. "You OK to eat?" he asked, seeing my somewhat lifeless form in the same position he'd left me, leaning on my left side, hand under my head, the other loosely clutching my right abdomen where the pain was prominent and still growing worse.

"Later," I replied, focusing back on the room's

little TV. "Arthur C. Clarke and Walter Cronkite." It was true, Dr. Clarke – my favorite author – was being interviewed by Cronkite, my favorite journalist. I would meet both of them in the coming 18 months, but right now I felt about done in. I waited until the show was over, and Rob had finished dinner.

"Guess I need to head for the hospital," I informed him.

"Ok," he said, more than prepared for this. "Do you think it's your appendix?"

"Hope so."

It most certainly was, but I knew there was more. At the ER, I was quickly ushered into a private room and greeted by a Dr. Yeo. He quizzed me on my symptoms, nodded, asked me for a urine sample, and when I couldn't produce one, he got it for himself. I couldn't believe I sat still to let him, or rather his nurse, do that. "Don't worry," he said. "Speaking as one guy to another, you just went through the worst, I guarantee it." His smile was reassuring.

A few minutes later, he came back into the room, Rob in tow. "Thought your friend might want to hear this, too, if that's OK."

"Yeah, of course."

"It's critical we get that appendix out right away. We're going to prep you for surgery." It was almost midnight.

"Can Rob go back to the motel?" But Rob was shaking his head, no.

"While we're in there, we want to do some exploration. See what's causing all these abdominal issues you've been having the past few months. You OK with that?"

"Mosquito bite," said the nurse who'd come back

into the room wheeling a tall device with a plastic bag full of liquid dangling from it. The needle was, in fact, a mere pinch as it entered my left arm. I saw the drip-drip-drip of liquid begin immediately. Guess my circulatory system was thirsty.

"Surgery?"

"Have you ever had a surgical procedure before?"

"No," I replied. "But now sounds like a good time for it."

"It is, before that appendix bursts," said Dr. Yeo.

The lights dimmed. "Rob, you can wait outside, or back at your motel." More people came into the room. They all wore white medical scrubs, and one of them leaned forward with a smile for me.

"Hey, chief," he said. "You ready?"

"I guess so."

"OK, I'm going to turn this knob," he said, pointing at the tall pole, which now had a second bag of liquid attached to it. "And you're going to go to sleep really, really fast."

"OK," I confirmed.

He turned it. "Count backward from ten." How the hell did this happen, I wondered.

"Ten, nine, eight, sev…"

"Keep counting," he encouraged.

"Sever…." I was going to keep counting, but I noticed then that many strange dots had appeared on the ceiling, and I thought it important to mention this to my medical team.

"Er…goo," was what I heard myself say.

I think they knew what I meant.

Then the lights really went out.

MODES OF ORIGIN

NORTHERN CALIFORNIA – 1967

It Came From Beyond

Never look a gift horse in the mouth.

"I found a dollar," said my older brother, Bill. "Let's go to the gas station."

For me, at age six, there could not be any better news. "Really? Where did you find it?" The look on his face said he'd prefer not to say, so I skipped to my next question. "But, how do we buy the candy without dimes?"

Bill was no dummy. He was nearly nine. "We ask the gas station guy to give us ten dimes for the dollar," he said. He was always the older, smarter brother. Ten dimes! That meant we could methodically extract ten candy bars, one at a time, from the gas station's vending machine. What a windfall!

I tried again. "Where did you find the dollar?" I asked.

"In plain sight." This answer completely satisfied my curiosity. It wasn't the first time Bill had found money, and it wouldn't be the last. We set out for the gas station, a thirty minute walk through our residential neighborhood.

The gas attendant gave us ten dimes. We enjoyed yanking the mechanical lever of the machine ten times. Each decision became more difficult, with an ever-diminishing number of options. Mounds. Mars. Almond Joy. Good and Plenty. Must choose wisely.

On the return home, as we approached the house, we both knew there was an elephant in the room: where would we find a safe hiding place for our horde? We'd eaten two each, and planned to finish the remainder that night or tomorrow. We entered our backyard through the gate and quickly observed that the bag of charcoal briquettes was nearly empty. Perfect. We stuffed the remaining candy into it, a brilliant hiding spot – in plain sight.

Mom came out just then. "Boys, let's clean up this messy yard." We scurried about, picking up balls, gloves, half-melted plastic green soldiers, and a dead lizard we'd been using as a dinosaur to attack the soldiers. "Ok, looking good, boys. Your dad just bought a new bag." She suddenly grabbed our briquettes bag candy stash.

"I'll throw that away, Mom," Bill volunteered. He was often helpful like that. He took the apparently empty bag, walked out of sight behind the house where the trash cans were kept, then tossed it lay-up style up onto the roof. It was a good toss -- just barely visible but not obvious.

We went inside. A few hours later, as dusk settled, we felt our sweet tooths stirring again. In the side yard, I was able to boost Bill onto the metal trash can. He could just barely reach it. We took turns digging into the bag to find goodies, our hands emerging black with coal dust but loaded with wrapped wonders of sweetness.

We heard the skid of the screen door opening on the far side of the house, where the barbeque was. Dad was home with the new charcoal and about to start the coals. Bill was taking no further chances, he grabbed out the last candy bars, said, "hide these in the gravel," then ran to the back fence and flung the empty charcoal bag over the fence into the neighbor's yard. I covered the remaining candy with gravel.

As we walked over to greet Dad, I whispered, "I think there might have been one more in there. The Good and Plenty." Bill stopped, looking mortified. It was his favorite candy.

"Boys," said Dad, "want to help start the fire?" We always did. An excessive amount of lighter fluid later, flames were leaping from the grill.

Something came spinning over the rear fence and landed with a plop next to the barbeque. The empty charcoal bag. "Hey!" said Dad. "Dang neighbor kids!" He walked into the kitchen to get cooking utensils.

We looked up at the fence. A blond haired, freckled boy's face and both arms were visible over the fence. He was chewing away. He poured more Good and Plenty from the box in his left hand and plopped it into his mouth.

"Who are you?" Bill asked.

"I'm Benny. I gave you your charcoal back."

"Where'd you get the candy?"

"Found it." We couldn't argue with that.

Dad came back out. "Hey," he barked, "Who took my dollar?"

NORTHERN CALIFORNIA – 1967

Fire Drill

Call for heroes only when you actually need heroics.

The shrill scream of an approaching emergency vehicle was growing louder. I had the sinking feeling it was coming for me. The cost of conducting science experiments has never been cheap.

As a kid, science was my thing. We happened to live next to one of the most accessible fossil quarries in the western United States, and I often walked there with my like-minded friends. We all badgered our parents until they bought us geology hammers. We'd go to Sliding Hill every Saturday and dig out ancient clamshells and fossilized plants.

That was, when we weren't messing around with our telescopes, microscopes, and chemistry sets. In those days, you could go to the toy store and buy Bunsen burners, Erlenmeyer flasks, and test tubes, along with assorted chemicals. I commandeered most of the bedroom I shared with my brother, Bill, and made it my personal chemistry lab.

Bill was kind of into it, too. Neither one of us could say later we were 100% proud of the experiments conducted there. Let's just say that we thoroughly verified the theory that a frog dropped in boiling water will instantly jump out. That's absolutely true. I'm afraid we also proved the reverse of that theory – that a slowly heated frog will expire through inaction.

So, perhaps no blame should accrue to my father for what happened when I attempted to verify that resin could be extracted from wood. It was something I called, "Wood Oil" and I meant to change the world with it. If I could extract a commercially usable portion of resin from a stick of wood, I figured that Standard Oil could be put out of business.

The problem was that the resin didn't accumulate much at boiling point temperatures. I needed something hotter. A fast distillation process would, I believed, give just enough extra temperature to extract resin. My set-up was simple: a test tube containing a stick and water hung above the burner of my alcohol lamp. The test tube had a cork with a hole in it where glass tubing was inserted, off which a flexible rubber hose ran to an Erlenmeyer.

After several failed experiments, I grew a bit frustrated. The wood wasn't being subjected to sufficient temperature. It was a risk, but I decided to expend a test tube (if necessary) by plugging it with cork. This would raise both the pressure and temperature. Best case: more resin. Worst case, the test tube would crack open.

As the alcohol-generated flame licked the test tube and built a black char coating on its hemispherical end, I got pretty excited. I could see a small coating of resin rising to the surface. The test tube was at a 45 degree angle, with the cork pointed safely away from the lab table toward the ceiling. Just to play it safe, I decided to retreat into the lab's blast shelter. This meant scooting behind a chair.

Very shortly after ducking, there was a loud pop-crack and an explosion of broken glass. That sharp jolt was followed by the tinkling of shards. It was a lot of glass.

I peeked from my hiding spot. The cork had held. But the bottom half of the test tube had ejected itself like a bullet, downward at 45 degrees. It had hit my one liter Erlenmeyer flask, a prized possession not available at the toy store; rather, I'd sweet-talked it from a retired chemistry teacher who'd had it sitting as décor in his living room. Probably irreplaceable.

It was a shattered mess. The flask had been hit at such velocity that it was reduced to shards. The open spigot was standing strangely by itself at a bizarre angle. Glass, boiling water, and "wood oil" was everywhere.

The bedroom door opened. My dad looked in, saw the mess, and closed the door. It seemed a smart move to me.

Ok, how to clean this up? The explosion had snuffed the alcohol lamp. I put on gloves and gingerly began to put jagged remnants in the trash can. That's when I heard the siren.

Sure enough, as the shrill noise grew to its peak volume, the vehicle rolled to a stop right in front of our house. The siren abruptly cut-out. I heard voices as men jumped from the vehicle and came up the drive to our house.

The fire captain entered the room. "OK in here?" he asked.

"Yeah," I said. "Is there a problem?"

He looked down the hall, presumably at my dad. "Your father says there was an explosion."

I don't remember much from there. I just remember telling the fireman and my dad that they had to let me try again.

But I do remember the last words the fireman said to my dad. "Sir, glad you played it safe, but you might want to take a more active role in your kid's science experiments. And don't call us until you see smoke."

Fire!

Here's a useful tip: don't play with matches.

There is nobody I can blame for it. Let's just agree on that now. When I was seven years old, my elementary school nearly burnt to the ground and I was involved.

We've already established that I can't blame anybody, so the first person I'm not blaming is my older brother, Bill. Now, I know what you're thinking: oh, big brother should know better. He most certainly did know better, and, unlike me, he didn't much care for school. If the school had been engulfed, most folks (and ours certainly) would have been pointing the finger at Bill. He was a well-known, and well-respected, prankster and troublemaker.

Still, he was nothing like the master neighborhood problem child, Benny. The moment the finger of accusation pointed at Bill, we all knew it would be a cakewalk for him to deflect it with a shrug of the shoulders, because hey, after all, it was Benny. Benny was the kid who actually DID put thumbtacks on the teacher's chair. When he left the principal's office after a dressing down he ALWAYS clicked his heels together, gave the principal a Nazi salute, and shouted "Javol, Mein Fuhrer!" whereupon he would be told to sit back down. He loved it, because he didn't have to go back to the classroom.

Benny loved TP'ing houses. Today we celebrate the rare occasion when a high schooler's parents awaken to find that the house has been toilet-papered in the wee hours of the night by his or her chums. "God love it," we'll say. "So good to see the children have not abandoned all of the traditions that made us who we are." And what are we if not befuddled adults digitally adrift from the young people in our lives?

Yep, no neighborhood judge or jury would hesitate to point the finger of indictment at Benny for virtually any transgression, should he be verifiably within a quarter mile of the incident at the time it occurred. Since Benny, Bill, and I had strolled over to the school together and left its premises together, Benny's prospects of acquittal in a court of law on the question of who burned down the school were scientifically estimable to be nil.

As a stern reminder of the opening paragraph, I agreed there is nobody upon whom I could lay the finger of blame for the near-conflagration. Had the school burnt, it would have been a life-changer for hundreds of kids and their parents, not to mention for the three of us. I shall hide no more. With my mildest of exposures to Catholicism and its keen sense of guilt – a blessing, by the way, of any religion worth its salt – there is in fact one at whom I can direct the finger of culpability for this disaster. One of the three of us. You will note that I have explicitly informed you that Bill and Benny are not to blame. My legal team, however, insists that I not actually disclose the name of the guilty party. So the finger-pointing must stop now.

Back to the story. It was a Saturday afternoon and we were bored as usual. Benny had jumped over the back fence between his yard and ours, and had begun terrorizing our cat. After we got him to agree that that wasn't cool, all three of us climbed into our treehouse. Within five minutes we all agreed there was nothing to do in the treehouse, except scare the cat by throwing coins and rocks at it when it happened to walk underneath. The cat was way too smart for that.

"I've got a book of matches," said Bill. "Let's go to the side of the school and light some on the dried weeds."

It was an inspired idea. None of us, to a man, could perceive any downside with this plan. Boredom would be banished.

The side yard of our school was a sequestered patch of very dry weeds. It was nearly summer break, and the days were hot. Bill pulled out the matchbook. "I'll go first," he said, and showed us how it was done.

He lit the match and flicked it into the weeds. Its little blue flame tumbled end over end, nearly vanished, then landed amidst the tall, ultra-dry foxtails. Within seconds, a blue glow and grayish smoke formed, then yellow fire grew into an expanding circle. Inside the expanding circle was black, burnt weed ash, and all around was fire. When the circle of fire reached about a foot in diameter, Bill stomped it out with a few well-placed footfalls.

"Your turn," he informed Benny.

Benny flicked long blond hair out of his freckled face, took the matchbook, and kneeled down into a fresh patch of dry weeds. He seemed to savor this opportunity. He lit the match and smiled as he held it nearly upside-down to develop the flame. Then he flicked it end-over-end several feet away.

The process repeated, the ring of fire growing larger every second. "Uh," said Bill. Benny waved him back; perhaps he had a vision of when to stomp. Another ten seconds passed, and the black, scorched circle was easily six feet in diameter when Benny began dancing with glee, landing his black combat boots over and over again. Bill and I joined in. At last, we snuffed out the fire. It took nearly thirty seconds. The blackened oval left behind was ten feet at its widest.

"Here you go, buddy," Benny said. "Think big!"

I took the matchbook. Bill and Benny were both more than two years my senior, so it was critical that I outshine them. I didn't actually need Benny's encouragement. I skipped the theatrics and just walked over to a fresh patch of fuel. It took me three tries, but just as in baseball, a homerun on the third pitch ain't no sin.

That sucker was burning and growing larger. At first both my accomplices noted their approval. Then Bill went quiet. "Burn, baby, burn!" cheered Benny. The ring of fire was easily twelve feet in diameter when I decided that youth had shown its superior chutzpah, and I began stamping. And stamping. And stamping. Bill jumped in, then Benny. We were stamping and laughing, until two of us weren't.

The ring of fire was still growing when I noticed that Bill and Benny were running. Benny was running in the general direction of his house. Bill was running toward the school's green, grassy field where a few kids and adults were playing baseball. I followed.

We arrived out of breath and informed an adult wearing an Oakland A's cap. "Sir, sir, there's a fire over there!" Bill informed him.

The man paused to look in the direction we were indicating. We turned with him. Yep, blue smoke was rising between the classroom bungalows. "Yeah? Ok, you should call the fire department." Then he continued his wind-up.

Bill muttered "Ok," and tore off toward home, a 90 second sprint; we got there in record time. "Mom! Mom! There's a fire at the school!"

Mom acted, as she always did, with complete presence of mind. "Show me." We dragged her to the curb. Down the street, beside the classrooms we inhabited Monday thru Friday the swirl of blue-gray smoke had grown larger, and darker. The fire was clearly accelerating. It was only a matter of minutes before it would reach and begin to burn the nearest classrooms and continue off on the other side. There was a wooden fence there, beyond which was a row of houses. Houses occupied by our neighbors and school mates.

"OK, I'm calling the fire department. You guys knock on those doors and warn them about the fire. And stay away from it." We did as instructed. We'd knocked on only three doors when we heard the sirens.

The fire truck screeched to a halt and within seconds that fire was vanquished. It had just begun licking at the wooden fence separating the school from the homes on whose doors we'd been knocking.

A crowd of neighbors gathered. The fire captain explained. "Just a little grass fire. No problem now. Did anyone see or hear anything that might have started this?"

The lump in my throat was so big that the Catholic-inspired mea culpa that I had intended to deliver was not coming out.

"Actually, no," said the first neighbor we'd stirred with that initial warning knock. "Our house is right here. Normally we hear kids goofing around behind the house, this time we didn't hear a thing."

"Hmm," said the fire captain.

"Yeah," said Bill, "we saw smoke and tried to tell the adults out there playing baseball. But they just told us to call the fire department, so we ran home and our mom called." Dang, if all that weren't the truth. Not the whole truth...

"You boys did good," said the captain. "This fire did no harm, thanks to your fast action."

"Thanks. Can we go home now?" Bill asked.

"Sure," said the fire captain. "Tell your mom thanks."

We did. For his part, that completely ended the affair for Bill. He never ceased to amaze.   I   felt the eyes of the firemen and the neighbors drilling into the backs of our skulls as we trotted home. They knew! There was no way they couldn't know. To me, the walk home was what today we call a "perp walk" with the difference being we'd got off scot free.

That night, ironically, we lit a barbeque in the backyard. I was totally sick with anguish over what I'd done and how close it had come to bringing chaos and potential tragedy to my neighbors. Getting away with it just made the guilt more painful. I was paralyzed with anxiety over the incident.

Not Bill. He was enjoying himself. After we lit the coals and they were flaring, he danced around the barbeque flicking the rest of his matches into the maelstrom.

"Hey, where'd you get those matches?" dad said.

"Found 'em at the scene of the fire." True!

SIERRA NEVADA MOUNTAINS, CALIFORNIA – 1974

Poor Richard

And one more tip: don't play with firearms.

The squirrel – either the most trusting or naïve to ever scamper across a forest floor – had paused several times already as it began crossing the range. It still had a long way to go to pass where our 22 caliber single-shot bolt-action rifles could easily take it down. We'd all seen it, all except the scoutmaster, who was in conversation with a park ranger who'd come by to chat.

Not a one of us boy scouts had any doubt about what we needed to do. First we needed to be quiet and keep shooting, so the scoutmaster wouldn't notice. More importantly, we needed to hit that squirrel. The scout who took it down would earn bragging rights.

There was a lot of pointing, but the only sounds we made now were the "pop! click! tinkle! clack!" that accelerated as we fired and re-loaded at a faster clip, shooting and re-working the bolts. The spent shell casings bounced off the redwood deck. The squirrel, undeterred, continued its innocent advance across the range just behind the line of posts that held our now very uninteresting concentric target grids.

It would scamper a few feet, then stop, and stand. Puffs of dirt erupted all around it, but damn us if we could shoot straight. The tension was thick, and we were all a bit jittery, which gave the squirrel a fighting chance. That critter was determined to keep going. It ran another few feet, halfway across. I'm not sure if it even could tell it was under assault.

"If that squirrel don't make it," the scoutmaster suddenly bellowed, "you're all going to be in the shithouse." A few of us got off one more quick shot, all of which missed. I lifted my barrel toward the sky. We all did. Game over.

Somewhere to my left there was one final click-tinkle-clack. I glanced over. It was Richard, and he was in a squat taking a final, careful bead on that poor rodent. "Goddammit, Richard!" yelled the scoutmaster.

"Pop!" A clean miss. The squirrel continued unscathed and finally disappeared into the forest. "Richard," said the scoutmaster, in the tone he often used when you could tell he meant to use Richard's diminutive nickname. There was no need to use it. Everyone knew he was a bit of a….well, he was Richard. "Lucky you're a shit-ass poor shot. You get KP duty tonight." Kitchen Patrol sounded glamorous, but it meant washing dishes for two hours.

Richard stood and grinned. He'd had KP every night so far.

Before dinner that night, there was an unexpected assembly outside the mess hall. The camp master, a stocky gray-haired man named Smoky who'd reportedly run the camp for more than 40 years, took off his ranger style hat and waved us into formation. He used his finger to "hush" us and soon the only sound was the familiar, and ever-present wheeze of the wind brushing through the trees. I'd grown to love the ceaseless music of these mountains.

"Gentlemen," said Smoky. "Before you bust into mess, I want you to know that we'll have the television on tonight." That was different. There was a single bulbous TV hanging on the wall, but we'd never seen it on.

"Something important is happening," he continued. "The President is giving a speech."

"They finally got tricky Dick!" someone shouted, to be rewarded with a few awkward laughs.

"You know as much as I do, gentlemen, but I suspect this is an historic night. Enjoy your chow. Dismissed!"

The chow tasted especially good. We couldn't really hear much of Nixon's speech, but it was clear that he was resigning the Presidency of the United States. I'd followed Watergate fairly avidly, and the only part that never made sense to me was why a President who was obviously going to win re-election would resort to such antics. It remains for me one of the mysteries of the universe.

That night, as our troop gathered around a small campfire to reflect on the day, as was custom for each of the many troops at camp, Richard — freshly back from his KP duty -- stood. He'd waited until our scoutmaster had left for the brief evening convocation of all the camp's scoutmasters. Richard had something to say, and this was obviously the moment.

"Look what I've got!" he said, holding up a single 22 caliber bullet.

"What are you gonna do with it?" one of the guys said, ensuring that all would agree that something absolutely had to be done.

"Throw it in the fire!" said another scout.

Richard waved him down. "I'm going to smash it with a rock on that tree stump. Of course, I'll point the bullet away from me."

"Allright!" There was much enthusiasm for this idea. I had serious reservations. I'd already had a few near misses with model rockets, and I understood something about the Newtonian concept of action-and-reaction. If the bullet flew away from Richard, the casing would likely fly toward him.

"Guys," I offered, "I don't think it works like that."

There was no stopping Richard. As he carefully placed the round on the tree stump and hefted a big rock to get the feel of it, I noticed that I wasn't the only one who understood basic physics. Most of the guys were backing away and shinnying up to trees for cover.

I got into the trees, and, for good measure, I hit the dirt.

Richard carefully brought the stone down hard on the stump.

"Pop!"

"Ow!" he cried. When I looked up, I saw Richard holding his left bicep. The troops emerged from shelter to see what he'd done to himself.

"Man, that was cool!" he said, but he wasn't letting go of his arm. Someone shone a flashlight on the situation. We could all see the blood. One of the guys sliced Richard's scout shirt with his pocket knife. A wash from a canteen showed a deep flesh wound. We put our scout training to work.

In First Aid, restore breathing, stop bleeding. Since he wouldn't shut up about how cool it was, we knew Richard was breathing just fine. One of the guys suggested "a neck tourniquet" but we settled on using Richard's uniform neckerchief to bound his arm tightly. He was definitely going to live, so we all agreed the scoutmaster would get a cover story.

"It was a bobcat! I fought it off with my knife."

He was quickly talked down to "I tripped and fell on a sharp rock."

The scoutmaster was back just as we finished. He didn't buy a word of our story, but let it go.

Poor Richard. It's not clear he learned a thing from any of this.

SOUTHERN CALIFORNIA – 1977

Special Orders

Fun and games during wartime can be hazardous.

At the moment in history that represented the pinnacle of the "Burger Wars" tensions were high. Global domination by a single fast food chain was now looking possible, if not a forgone conclusion. The competition, who were struggling mightily to create their own burger clowns and equivalents to the Golden Arches, were on the highest state of alert. Spies, espionage, and predatory recruitment of employees and customers were common.

In hindsight, perhaps, it was not the most auspicious time for my friends and me to do what we did that one summer night, particularly as we lived in L.A., ground-zero for the titanic clash of the burger giants. Still, someone thought of it, and all of us were laughing, and we were ready to give it a try.

Not for a moment did any of us think it might be dangerous.

We'd only recently begun driving, and drive-through fast-food was still a big deal. The sun had set, and we'd just picked up some burgers, fries, and sodas at McDonald's, when we realized they had given us one too many cheeseburgers.

Rather than haggling over which of the four of us would devour it, one of the guys said: "Let's drive through the other McDonald's and sell it back to them!"

That sounded like fun. We pulled up to the ordering box, which emitted a staticky "May I take your order please?"

Our driver, Randy, put his hand over his mouth and tried to emulate the sound. "We'd like to sell you one cheeseburger."

"I'm sorry," came the scratchy response, "what was that?"

"Cheeseburger," he repeated, no more clearly.

"Please drive forward to the window." He did. When the girl there reached out for payment, he handed her the bag containing the cheeseburger from the first McDonald's and said, "that'll be 39 cents plus tax." The girl took the bag, and opened her mouth.

That's when Randy burnt rubber to get us out of there. We were definitely having fun now. Just a few blocks away was a Jack-In-The-Box. We pulled into the drive-through and could see no other cars in line.

As we crept up slowly on the ordering box, someone suggested we sing the Burger King jingle. "May I take your order?" came the serious monotone robotic voice of a male attendant.

Randy silently counted down on fingers – one, two, three! Then all four of us, in chorus, unrehearsed, blasted into song: "Hold the pickles, hold the lettuce, special orders don't upset us, all we ask is that you let us serve it your way." We were cracking up, until we started the final chorus. "Have it your way, have it your way at—"

"Crap!" said someone in the back seat.

A man wearing fast food white was now charging up the drive-through from the front of the restaurant. He was walking fast and looked really, really angry. Fortunately, there was no one behind us.

"Back-up!" I shouted.

Randy threw the car in reverse, did a Y turn, and sped to the driveway from where we'd entered. There was traffic: he had to stop. "You better go, Randy, he's coming!"

The man was bearing down on our vehicle. The look on his face said it all: *you've crossed the line and now you'll pay!*

Finally, an opening. Randy put the spurs to his 1970 Dodge Dart. The vengeance-seeking burger seller, seeing his prey about to escape, leapt forward and slapped the trunk hard. The noise was like a thunderclap. Then the car was moving down the street.

We were all four of us momentarily quiet. "That guy takes his job way too seriously," someone said. "Seems special orders can be very upsetting."

WASHINGTON, D.C. – 1977

But Then We'll Have to Kill You

That's right, walk in like you own the place. You pay taxes.

We had a lot going on that third day in D.C. The next two hours were elective time outside the group agenda, and Chris and I had a strong interest in aerospace. There was a hearing about to start on the second floor of the Dirksen Building called "Extending Practical Impact of LANDSAT Earth Sciences."

Chris and I found Room 221B, and walked in. There were a dozen men and one woman in business suits seated at four tables that formed a rectangle. They were just finishing lunch. There were plenty of chairs, so we quietly seated ourselves at one side of the room. I opened my notebook to record any key points made in the discussion.

It hadn't quite started yet, which was a little awkward. By way of breaking the ice, one gentleman walked to the trashcan to toss his paper plate, then came over say hello to us.

"Well, good afternoon," he said. "I'm Dan Fink." We shook hands and introduced ourselves.

"Very nice to have you here," he continued. "Are you two interns?"

"No, we're with Capital Classroom." We had to explain what that was.

"High school students! Well, very good, I'm sure you're learning a lot here in our nation's capital, just as I am."

"Are you a Congressman?" Chris asked.

"No," said Dan, "I'm the Vice President of General Electric. I don't know much about this town either." He smiled. Another suited figure stood behind a podium and was clearing his throat. Dan waved and went back to his seat.

"Gentlemen," said the speaker, "we've about done the LANDSAT environmental agenda to death. I thought we'd get started now on military applications." He garnered 100% attention.

"Imaging down to one meter resolution, as we discussed, gives us some unique capabilities to peek into places we haven't previously been able to observe. I'm going to put up a slide here..." The lights dimmed, and on a broad projection screen we saw an image form. "That's actually one of the Chinese silos. We can confirm based on this..." another slide, taken from ground level, "which you can see shows the same outlines."

Directly across from Chris and me, two more men leaned in toward each other and began whispering. One pointed in our direction. I turned my gaze back to the speaker, but I sure had a feeling something was up.

I could see them whisper back and forth for a few more seconds, then one of them stood quietly and came around the table to us. He smiled.

"Pardon me, gentlemen," he said quietly, "which Congressman are you paging for?"

We just pointed to our Capital Classroom badges.

"Ah, got it. Do you mind coming with me?"

We followed him into the hallway. "Terribly sorry," he said, "This is a closed hearing requiring security clearance. Our mistake, we thought you were part of the group when you came in."

"No problem," I said, "but is it possible to continue auditing the discussion? We're very interested in this topic."

He laughed, not unkindly. "No, afraid not. Not that we think you're spies or anything, it's just....the rules."

"We understand," said Chris. With that the man slipped back inside Room 221B and gave us a little salute as he shut the door.

"I believe we just crashed our first classified briefing," said Chris.

"Come on," I said. "I'm sure we can find more of these." We headed down the halls to find our next confidential trespass.

WASHINGTON D.C. – 1977

No Nukes Is Good Nukes

It's wise to prioritize.

We made good time charging down the Mall after visiting the Smithsonian Air and Space Museum, headed back toward the Capitol dome. We chanced upon a rather attractive young woman, likely college aged, in front of a little table with a sign that read, "Take Control of Our Nuclear Future." This was interesting, so when she greeted us, we paused to learn more.

"Hi!" she said. "We're here on behalf of Lyndon LaRouche. Would you like to sign our petition?"

"What are you guys trying to do?" I asked.

She began a quick diatribe all about the horrors of our modern nuclear age. I could totally get that at first, but as she continued I became increasingly skeptical by what I was hearing.

"These big capitalist corporations are threatening our existence by building nuclear power plants in every state of our nation. They don't care one whit about the horrible environmental damage, mutations to babies, and high incidence of cancer their technology is perpetrating upon our nation. If one of these plants should blow up, it would destroy a large fraction of the country."

"So," I said, "you are focused on stopping commercial nuclear energy generation?"

"That's right," she affirmed, "for all the reasons I just mentioned and so many more."

"Do you do anything against nuclear proliferation?" asked Chris, looking at the petition he held in his hand, and which he was not yet close to signing.

"We're absolutely fighting the proliferation of these big corporate killers, like Bechtel and Westinghouse."

"Hmm," Chris said.

"Don't you think nuclear weapons are a bigger threat to humanity than fission based energy generation plants?" I asked, in what I thought was a reasonable question.

"Oh, I see," she said. "You guys don't get it. You're on their side."

"Actually," said Chris, "not necessarily. I'm still trying to understand what it is that you are trying to accomplish."

"Well, think about this…" she said. "If a plant is built near you and you breathe in a single atom of plutonium, you'll die of lung cancer."

Neither Chris nor I were nuclear physicists. Nor were we doctors. Still, for the sake of all that's sane and good about America's youth, we'd actually read a few issues of Scientific American.

"Now, you know," said Chris, very carefully, "that the half-life of plutonium is something like 20,000 years?"

"See! The poison remains forever," she concluded.

"Actually," I said, "it diminishes with time. Arsenic is forever."

"Like that matters!" she said.

"Well, in fact," Chris explained, "I think it does. You said one atom. I'd have to live to be approximately 20,000 years old before that one atom would have a 50/50 chance of decaying and releasing an alpha particle."

"Which might," I added, helpfully, or so I thought, "or might not chance into a cell in say the alveoli of his lung, mutate that cell in just the right way to make it a cancer cell, which would then take a few more years to run rampant in his body, before killing him."

"You guys want to support death," she proclaimed. "That's your choice."

"Can we at least agree on the hazards of the fusion bomb?" I offered.

The conversation, however, had been terminated.

We continued our fast-walk down the Mall toward the Capitol. "I'm not sure we won the argument," I said to Chris.

"No, we lost," said Chris. "Anytime you bring facts and priorities to a mud-wrestle, you're bound to lose."

SOUTHERN CALIFORNIA – 1979

Pseudoscience

Mixing science and religion could be fun. Or annoying.

I've always been a ravenous reader. No subjects completely repel me, but I particularly love the sciences and science fiction – the harder the better in both cases.

Notwithstanding the foregoing, my mind is open to realms beyond provable science. In my teens I read lots of books about the Bermuda Triangle, ancient astronauts, and UFOs. One of my favorites is *Flying Saucers – Serious Business!* Check it out sometime.

For the record, I'm a strong believer in UFOs – I have seen Unidentified Flying Objects. I also believe in aliens – do the math, they are definitely out there. I just don't believe for a millisecond that I have seen a UFO that had anything to do *with* aliens. If you think the oceans are vast and mysterious, the skies are a lot bigger. While "they are out there," that doesn't mean they are running around Earth, much less being craftily hidden away inside Cheyenne Mountain by the vast Dark Government Conspiracy.

In the spirit of exploring the edges and frontiers of science, I chanced across a book when I was 19 that was so compelling, I simply had to read it. Maybe it wasn't even chance. After all, I knew the author very well. A long time back he had actually been a damned good science fiction writer.

The story of how L. Ron Hubbard came to found the Church of Scientology should be legendary. Note to Hollywood: this is one of the last great true stories that has yet to be released as a blockbuster. No, I would not suggest casting Tom Cruise. Not the way the real script ran.

L. Ron and some of his fellow science fiction writers got together regularly in a bar in New York City, back in the late 1940s and early 1950s. They talked shop, but mostly they argued about absolutely everything, which, to me, is the most fun you can have in a bar. The story goes that one evening the topic of religion came up. L. Ron made a bold claim:

"Starting a religion is an easy way to get super-rich." His fellow writers completely pooh-poohed this proposition. People aren't stupid, they argued. You can't just start something and expect people to fall into it like zombie automatons and start shelling out their cash. "The hell you can't," he responded. "And I'm going to prove it."

He'd already published a book called *Dianetics: The Modern Science of Mental Health*. He decided to build on that for his religion. The rest, as they say, is history.

Dianetics was a compelling proposition for me: while I knew it had been the genesis of a somewhat obtuse religious order, the premise was fascinating. It's a book dancing on the edges of both science and spirituality that is also arguably a "self-help" book about how to get control of your own mind. I dug into it. Six hundred pages later, I have to say I was impressed: the concept of "engrams" – bubbles of memory formed in our youngest days – was fascinating.

The book argued that we all had many "negative engrams" – memories of unhappy events that we didn't always know were there, but that drove our everyday behavior. A careless babysitter who scalded our feet in too-hot bathwater, while we couldn't remember it specifically, might make us cranky toward baths the rest of our lives. You get the idea.

I finished the book and found a little postage paid card in the back asking: "Want more information about Dianetics and how to exercise your negative engrams?" Well, in fact I did. So I filled it out and put it in the mail.

That proved a huge mistake.

Within a week I got a letter. In those days, it was not unusual for me to actually send and receive letters in the U.S. Mail. This one was hand-written in lovely cursive by a young woman named Jennifer. She wrote effusively about how Scientology had turned her life around, and how she hoped I would join the church, and that perhaps we could meet for coffee.

Now, as a geeky teenaged guy, it occurred to me that I should dial the phone number she wrote at the end, complete with little smiley faces for the zeroes, and meet this intriguing new friend. Except, I was aghast, maybe even a little frightened. What kind of organization whips its people into a recruitment frenzy such that they approach random strangers with laboriously handwritten letters?

In any case, I didn't have the least interest in Scientology, though I had plenty of interest in the essential theories of Dianetics. I decided to explore some other similar books, and tossed the letter in the trash.

In the meantime, for the next six months or more, the handwritten letters kept coming. They were not just from Jennifer, but from other young women. I ignored these too. At some point I started getting the same kind of letters from young men. Obviously, they thought I might fit a different profile. These letters went into the trash unopened.

In hindsight, it might have been nice to keep a few as curiosities. L. Ron Hubbard proved his point and became immensely wealthy. He also kept writing science fiction, though the quality of his novels degraded seriously and hit rock-bottom with the publication of *Battlefield Earth*. Later, a famous actor played a major character in the horrifically poor movie version of this novel. His name was John Travolta. Lucky for him, his career was rescued by another young science fiction geek living in L.A.

But that's another story.

SOUTHERN CALIFORNIA – 1979

Another Story

Meeting celebrities before they become famous is a thing.

The late 1970s and early 1980s were the heyday of big science fiction conventions. At a time when Comic-Con was a backwater event in San Diego, L.A. hosted waves of big cons that drew top luminaries from the science fiction literary, television, and cinema universes.

At one of the after-hours parties that formed up in a convention hotel suite, I joined friends and strangers alike one evening, nearly all of us in costume. I hadn't learned how to drink yet, but the atmosphere was so convivial I remember sipping a beer.

There's something you should know about the most hardened science fiction fans. They tend to see people as falling into one of two camps: you're either a Fan or you're a Mundane. Now that's not a bad thing, but it is a thing. Most of us had friends and family who fell squarely into the Mundane camp – ok, almost everybody we knew outside of these events were Mundanes. The chief flaw of Mundanes is that they simply don't get it. They don't get the sweep of the stars, our astounding predicament of living on a tiny pebble in space, or even how cool it is that Spock has no emotions. Still, Mundanes have their place. No, they don't appreciate science fiction the way we do, but, hey, vive la difference.

In point of fact, Fandom draws more than its fair share of the immature, under-socialized, maladjusted and egotistical, and way more than its fair share of introverts. Yet, when you put hundreds or thousands of Fans together in one place, the casual observer might be shocked by the public displays of emotion and biting debates. Even the most timid Fan may be drawn into loudly singing 'filk songs' (folk songs written about Fandom subjects) or gallivanting through hotel lobbies and conference rooms in ad hoc re-enactments of scenes from their favorite movies and TV shows.

In a more innocuous example I can recollect, several of my friends and I marched through the halls of the L.A. Bonaventure Hotel while loudly singing the words "Para-dimethyl amino benzaldehyde!" over and over again to the tune of *The Irish Washerwoman*, ending the song loudly with the triumphant statement of "2-3 trans-dibromo-isobutane!" If you have no idea why we might do this, I highly recommend Isaac Asimov's essay, *You, too, Can Speak Gaelic*. We sang and marched so ardently you'd think we were recently liberated French people singing La Marseillaise.

In the open, accepting environment of a science fiction convention, Fans tend to be highly opinionated and are not shy about giving voice -- loudly -- to their beliefs. These events can bring out some very aggressive behavior from these ordinarily passive individuals. That makes some of them appear to be complete jerks.

At this particular party, there was a skinny guy wearing a Sandman costume. Sandmen are the enforcers from the book (and movie) *Logan's Run*, in which a youthful society is kept that way by the ritualistic extermination of people as they reach a certain age -- in the film version, those turning 30 were expected to willingly consign themselves. Those who refuse to die in the ritual and chose to "run" are deemed "Runners" and they are hunted down and blasted to bits by the Sandmen.

This particular skinny Sandman was not wearing a blaster. He was standing alone holding a white Styrofoam cup. Occasionally, he would walk up to a group of people and start talking. I noticed after half an hour that he'd done this repeatedly, and that each time the group would soon start to look at their watches and disperse, leaving him standing alone again. I felt sorry for him, and, having perhaps a little bit of a beer buzz, I sauntered up and complimented his costume.

He responded with something dismissive about mine. Never to be put-off so easily, I asked him what he thought of Logan's Run.

"It's a great idea we should evaluate as a society," he said. "Especially for the Mundanes."

Before I could respond, a group of friends sidled up and one of them yanked on my black cape.

"Dude," he whispered in my ear. "Trust me, you don't want to get into it with Quint."

That wasn't his real name. Although at the time Quint was a socially-awkward video store rental clerk in the L.A. area, he later became globally famous for making innovative movies -- often featuring scenes of sudden violence.

I whispered back to my friend: "What do you mean, 'don't get into it'?" I had no idea what they were talking about, but my friend gave me a stern look that indicated he was quite serious. I nodded to Quint and dutifully followed my friend into another section of the room. "OK," I badgered him. "Now what's the deal with Quint?"

"Don't ask," said another friend. "Let's just say he's twisted and has a way of freaking people out."

Turns out those characteristics can be very valuable – at least in Hollywood. And in hindsight, I wish I *had* "gotten into it" with Quint. He was one Fan whose abrasive nature must have been an asset when he pursued his dreams. He did OK for himself.

SOUTHERN CALIFORNIA – 1980

Endangered Species

Being an environmentalist does not conflict with one's need to be the center of attention.

"Save the whales!" It was a message my friend Rob and I could get behind as it gained traction during our first year of college. Soon, however, it was feeling a little over-played.

"Whales are great," noted Rob. "Blue Whales are the largest creatures to have ever existed on our planet. On top of that, whales are vastly intelligent."

"I disagree with that latter point," I said. "Sure, they communicate in a song-language we can't understand; but if they're so smart, why are they being hunted to extinction by other creatures who enjoy eating blubber? If you're going to be so great and be hunted out of existence, it should be because you taste like a hot fudge sundae, or something."

Rob considered my observation carefully for the few milliseconds his immense intellect required. I'd always been proud to have friends like Rob – far more intelligent than I, but who seemed to put up with a lower order intellect like myself, primarily – I believed – because of my arbitrary statements that they enjoyed de-coding.

"Your inane comment has some merit," he allowed. "One whale contains enough nutrition to feed hundreds of people. They've been around a lot longer than homo sapiens, so if they could control their evolution, they probably should have worked at developing opposable thumbs so they could hunt humans for sport. I assume we, too, taste crappy."

This observation was revelatory. "Sharks don't care for us," I said. "Yes, they're ancient fish, not mammals, but poor taste translates across genus, I suspect." I think I meant phylum or kingdom instead of genus, but Rob didn't argue the point.

"Look," I continued, "there's nothing sacred about big animals versus small, or smart animals versus dumb. Every species is unique."

"True. Although the merits…"

"The merits?" I pressed on. "Is the mosquito, pest that it is and infested with disease, not unique?"

"Hmm." Rob pondered, but only for a few milliseconds. "We stand atop the food chain and reserve the right to exterminate pests."

"That seems tacitly amoral," I proclaimed. "Where do you draw the line on pestilence? The bee that stings, yet pollinates? Seems counterproductive. The common house fly? Much easier to engineer the meshed screen than swat them all into extinction."

"Flies are largely harmless; mosquitoes regularly kill with malaria."

Silence for Rob and me was never golden. It meant that both of us were at a loss at the exact same time. It seemed to drag on.

"Scabies," I said. "Where do you draw the line

on scabies?"

If you've never had scabies, try to keep it that way. Scabies are tiny bugs that burrow in the space below the skin and above deep tissue. They are, in the words of Douglas Adams, "mostly harmless," but they create ugly lines on the skin and itch like crazy. So I'd been told. By my older brother, who caught scabies. Before he infected me.

Rob's vast intellect rendered its verdict. "Savable. Scabies should not be exterminated just because they are annoying." More silence, while we both pondered this. It made sense. It was a solid line to draw in the sand – which species should be saved, and which should be eradicated for the common good? We assessed that that fine line was drawn at scabies. Before long, to communicate this important message to our fellow environmentalists and college students, we had shirts made. They were black t-shirts with big bold white letters that said: "SAVE THE SCABIES".

Some people loved the shirts. Some clearly thought that we were over the top. In hindsight, I'm not proud, but I am pleased to note that scabies continue to thrive. I believe this is in no small part due to our efforts, facts to the contrary be damned.

In any case, we did make the shirts.

LOS ANGELES – 1980

Spooking the Secret Service

The men and women of this elite team must be flexible.

In October, 1980 there was yet another big science fiction convention in Los Angeles. This one was at the Airport Hilton, and my friends and I planned to camp out for the full three days, five to a room. In fact, my circle of science fiction friends had grown so much, that there would be many other rooms over-stuffed with enthusiastic fans, almost all of whom wore costumes and carried "hardware" – props like Luke Skywalker's Lightsaber, Mr. Spock's Tricorder, and of course Captain Kirk's Phaser.

The science fiction world was never pure. Comic books, Dungeons and Dragons, and Renaissance Faire were represented, as well as Fantasy – Tolkien, Terry Brooks, and Zelazny's Avalon. Fantasy hardware invariably meant swords, many of which were actually forged by their owners, who wore them proudly during the convention.

On top of that, this year many folks had gone the Galactica route. The show was far from my cup of tea, but the uniforms were of undeniably outstanding design, and the black blasters, worn wild-west fashion in holsters, were pretty slick. Many of these featured battery powered LEDs and 'laser' noise makers. It was all very cool.

Something else was happening in October 1980 – the presidential election. A certain former governor of California was running on the Republican ticket. For some reason, he was scheduled to give a speech at the Hilton while our convention was going on.

On the morning of day two, a number of us were clustered for breakfast at a table in the Hilton coffee shop. I wore my usual costume, which was of my own design and not representative of any particular science fiction universe – black long sleeves, a silvery plastic torso that was supposed to deflect laser attack, black cape and knee-high boots.

My friend Christopher was lithe in his Galactica uniform. He had had it tailored with help from his girlfriend, and it was sharp. More impressive was the blaster at his side. The thing looked positively lethal. He could draw it from its holster and fire simulated blaster bolts faster than Doc Holliday. Each trigger pull sounded like staccato gunshots with an electronic "twang!" and bright flash -- it was quite dramatic.

The coffee shop was crowded, and not just with Star Trek and Star Wars characters. Dotted around the large dining hall were six or seven tables each seating two to four men wearing business suits. They all looked the same. They had short hair and dark glasses. Each one of them had a single earbud attached to a wire that disappeared beneath their collars.

We knew they were Secret Service.

The booth immediately adjacent to us had three

such men, and we could almost make out their mumbling words. To be honest, we didn't try. We were having too much fun. But these fellows were taking an increasing interest in our conversation which was goofy, far-ranging, and loaded with science fiction code words. Given our costumes and lethal looking props, and the fact that the possible next president of the United States might stride into the hotel premises at any moment, they might have been just a little spooked.

Christopher, no Republican, took note of their attention. He started to talk more loudly. "You know, I hear there's going to be a special visitor coming here today. Nothing to do with our event."

"Oh, and who would that be?" I played along.

"I believe his name is Ronald." He slid his blaster out of its holster, and laid it gently, harmlessly, on our table. "Ronald RAY GUN."

The guys in suits had stiffened when the prop appeared. Now they all began to laugh. One of them lifted his dark glasses and gave us a wink. Then they completely ignored us and finished their breakfast.

We missed the whole Reagan visit and speech that occurred in a large conference room at the hotel about an hour later. Probably for the best.

FIAWOL

Fandom Is A Way Of Life. Science Fiction Fandom, that is.

At the very next of these big L.A. science fiction conventions, in early 1981, a civil war was breaking out. Emotions ran raw in the hallways and conference events, perhaps with the tension many felt by the imminent inauguration of Ronald Reagan; perhaps not. Maybe it was the Iranian hostage crisis. Whatever the reason, nowhere did these emotions swell more than in the dealer room.

At any recreational convention, there is always a healthy dealer concession filled with fans who are also merchants. They ply their trade in everything from pulp copies of Astounding Stories magazine to hand-crafted blasters and incredibly well-rendered painting, sculpture, and other artwork. Everything has a science fiction or fantasy bent, of course.

Most of the merchants, as usual, were seriously dyed-in-the-wool Fans, the type who dedicate their lives to Fandom. Most had day jobs, but they lived for the Cons, the camaraderie of fellow Fans, the next major book, and cinema releases. In a simpler, less sensitive time, these folks were labeled as "geeks." They wore that mantle with no insult.

Though they themselves held such name-callers in complete contempt. They labeled those who tossed around the term "geek" or "sci-fi freak" as "Mundanes." To be called a Mundane in the world of science fiction fandom was a mortal insult – assuming the recipient recognized its implications. "Mundane was the "M-word" of science fiction; no joke.

A new clique of Fans seemed to be rising that made their presence known at this Con in powerful ways not previously seen. For example, science fiction fans can be both conservative and liberal. At this convention, the conservative wing of the science fiction party was flexing its muscles. Jerry Pournelle, a versatile and accomplished author and critically noted conservative voice, was featured prominently in many of the panel discussions.

The divide was not cleanly along political lines. The only clear schism was between those who believed Fandom Is a Way of Life (FIAWOL), and those who believed with equal passion that Fandom is Just a God Damned Hobby (FIJAGDH). These two camps, the Sunni and Shia of the science fiction world, seemed to be coming to blows at this convention. An ominous premonition of violence hung in the air.

In fact, it did come to blows. There were heated debates and arguments in the dealer room. It seemed for a time that one side or the other would, horror of horrors, call the other side Mundanes. Some of the dealers were talented blacksmiths selling exquisitely long and sharp deadly broadswords. Fortunately, these were not employed as the chosen instruments of conflict.

Instead, to their immense credit, the warriors of FIAWOL and FIJAGD in the end realized that, despite their differences, both sides were indeed human.

Yet honor called, battle would have to be joined. Two ad hoc leaders, one of each faction, came to the fore mostly through their clear-headed senses of humor. They were able to work out a field of valor that would enable the One True Faith of science fiction to be demonstrated once and for all. Much as Captain Kirk and the Gorn leader settled the fate of their inter-species rivalry through single combat (see the original Star Trek episode "Arena"; better yet, read the Damon Knight story on which it's based), they decided to choose five warriors each from their respective factions.

That night, they engaged in full-out elimination combat, in which only one of the ten warriors could remain "alive." That one would represent the one legitimate faction. Either FIAWOL or FIJAGDH would emerge alone as the One True Way of Fandom.

So it was that the six story parking structure of the LAX Marriott Hotel became the Battleground Royale, the Hunger Games arena of an earlier day. Combat ensued. No mercy was on offer and no quarter was given as the two teams fired their weapons and maneuvered for supreme advantage.

Needless to say, the combat broke down into complete melee. Too many people of both factions, and far more of neither, were watching and enjoying the antics. They didn't come to this Con unarmed, so they joined in. The air filled with rubber darts, the percussive "whang!" of the spring-loaded projectiles echoed off the concrete walls of the parking structure. The whole business degraded into a dart gun party that went into the wee hours. The few Mundanes who were actually trying to park or find their cars were respectfully left-alone, and the night passed without incident.

In the morning, all had had a whopping good time, and absolutely nothing had been settled. Most outside observers would say about the whole FIAWOL vs FIJAGDH conflict that it really didn't matter.

Both sides were freaking crazy geeks.

May they always remain so. FIAWOL! I mean, FIJAGDH!

ADVENTURE MODE

ROSEBURG, OREGON – 1981

Awakenings

*How the hell did **this** happen?*

"Eisenhower is dead." That's the first thing I remember saying after waking from surgery. I just had no idea why I would say such a thing.

I perceived Dr. Yeo's head nodding in assent against a backdrop of bright hospital fluorescent lights. "True," he affirmed. "But he died from other causes. Do you eat margarine, cook a lot with Crisco?"

I shut my eyes again to think about that. A long time later, after a brief, dreamless snooze, I re-opened them.

"Hey, chief," said Dr. Yeo. "You did good. Can you hear me now?"

"Yes," I said, annoyed that he thought to ask.

"Great. I was talking earlier, don't think you were quite with us. My shift is over, but I wanted to let you know what we found."

"OK," I said, not really caring about what they found, but mildly concerned that the doctor was going to leave.

109

"So again, good news, we got the appendix out before it burst. It was a very near thing. You know when that happens, you could go into septic shock and it's very complicated and risky."

"That's good."

"Now we did find you have some Crohn's Disease." Later, I would appreciate the irony of his use of the word 'some.' "That's what got your appendix inflamed and what's been causing your nausea and pain the last few months."

"What's Crohn's?"

"It's something of a mystery, actually. President Eisenhower had it."

"He's dead," I observed again. I heard a few laughs from two nurses who courteously found this amusing the second time.

"Right, Crohn's isn't likely to kill you. Though it could. It can be extremely painful, though. We know it's your own immune system attacking your gut – everything from here," he gestured at his throat, "through your digestive tract all the way down."

"What's the cause?"

"That's the mysterious part. Do you eat a lot of margarine?"

Nothing was making sense – the bright lights, the generalized pain, the tubes I perceived running into and out of various places in my body, but the doctor – he was making a lot of sense; too much sense. How could he know to ask this question, and why?

I was a college student who had only recently moved out of my mother's house, and thus I had begun shopping and cooking for myself. Butter? She used it on everything, but it was expensive. Margarine was dirt cheap. I'd been consuming it by the pound for over a year.

"The big science on Crohn's was a study done on the population of Germany from before the rise of Hitler – poor economy – until after the war. Ironically, the economy was good during Hitler's rule. Before and after, Crohn's incidence in Germany was very high. During the war years, it plummeted. The isolated factor: margarine. Germans gave it up during the good times in favor of butter, and the incidence of Crohn's retreated. Margarine, which has inferior proteins for building cell walls, appears to make us vulnerable to autoimmune disease."

"I'll never touch the stuff again," I said.

"That's good. Were it so simple. Once you've got Crohn's it's for life. So when you get home to Southern California, you'll want to see a gastroenterologist. I'll check in on you when I come back tonight. You're going be here a good week or so."

"Thanks, doc," I said. "A week?"

"Or so."

When I left, nine days later, I was 20 pounds lighter and considerably changed. For the first time, I'd let my beard grow. I recovered from the surgery, but not entirely. Things were happening in my gut, and they weren't pleasant. On the day I left the hospital, the nurse encouraged me to eat my first solid food – breakfast. It didn't taste like much.

I was taxied to a bus station, staggered aboard, rode two hours to Medford, found an airplane there and flew to Long Beach. All at great expense, which my grandparents had covered for me, since as a college student, I didn't really have much money.

My job, college, science fiction, hobbies, the

concept of dating girls and the whole idea of eating anything were no longer on my priority list. I wanted to know what this Crohn's thing was, and how I was going to beat it.

LONG BEACH, CALIFONIA – 1981

Life Can't Get Better

With Inflictakil™.

"Sulfa what?" I asked. My gastroenterologist, Dr. Ahmad, nodded his head emphatically in the affirmative.

"Oh, yes," he said. "Sulfasalazine. You'll need to take it four times a day."

"OK," I said. "How long do I need to take it?"

He gave me a puzzled look, as if I hadn't understood a word of what he was trying to tell me. "The rest of your life, of course. You don't want to get sick again."

"Forever? How does it work?"

"It will reduce inflammation, so your symptoms won't be as prevalent."

"You mean I won't know when I'm getting sick again?"

"Look," he tried to reason, "you'll do much better on this drug. You can avoid more surgeries."

He hadn't answered my question satisfactorily. In my mind, it sounded like a way to hide the fact that

I was getting sick, yet it wouldn't do a thing to prevent the sickness. What he hadn't said, but which I already knew without acknowledging, was that the medical community considered Crohn's to be a permanent chronic fact of life that would plague and slowly eat out the guts of the sufferer – from rectum to esophagus, it was all at risk.

"Look," I told him. "I'll take this bottle home with me."

"Good."

I opened the child-protective screw cap and looked inside. The pills were horse-sized, flaming yellow, the color of sulfur. They smelled like sulfur. Sulfasalazine.

"I'll take it home," I repeated. "But I seriously doubt I'll ever take a single one of these things."

He was a good doctor. He shook his head in frustration. "You're the boss. I can only tell you what the medical community recommends."

This was the early 1980s, and the FDA had not yet decreed that Big Pharma had to loudly advertise all side-effects of their curative formulas.

But if they had, I could well imagine this one.

An attractive mid-twenties woman is walking into the gym, smiling and waving to a handsome male friend lifting weights.

Narrator: "Crohn's Disease – you're not going to control where and when we defecate anymore; now, *we* get to decide. That's right, with Inflictakil™, Life Can't Get Better. Take control of your Crohn's symptoms. With just four carefully timed doses per day, you're back in charge at the toilet."

The young woman enters a Zoomba class already in motion, and joins the fun with a powerful lunge, gripping her big toe as it sneaks up from behind her. "Inflictakil™ can cause drowsiness, so don't operate heavy machinery or drive while taking Inflictakil™. Powerful medicine for people who want to take the power away from their Crohn's.

"Feelings of impending doom and frequent night terrors are common side-effects. See your clinical psychotherapist if these persist beyond the first two years of usage. Anal hemorrhage, bouts of nausea, and vomiting may occur; see your doctor.

"Inflictakil™ should be taken only on a full stomach. Skipping or doubling doses has been known to cause amniobalactic neural discharge, which can lead to irreversible brain damage. Temporary or permanent paralysis should be treated immediately."

The woman quips with a friend while drying sweat with her towel. In the background, another woman is seen urgently dashing into the ladies room. Both friends roll their eyes and erupt in joyous laughter.

"Pregnant women intending to birth live offspring should avoid taking Inflictakil™. Get a grip on your lavatory habits with powerful medicine.

"Wrenching intestinal pain, massive uncontrollable diarrhea, and weeks-long bouts of constipation accompanied by projectile vomiting and dehydration should be reported to your medical professional promptly. Spontaneous human combustion leading to city-wide firestorms that leave no survivors are seldom reported with Inflictakil™.

"Inflictakil™ and your Crohn's. Life can't get better."

When I got home that afternoon, I tossed the bottle of giant yellow pills into the trash. I never took another pill for treatment of Crohn's. Instead, I try to stay calm and never eat hydrogenated anything. And to the best of my knowledge, I've never spontaneously combusted.

I derive a sense of pride from that.

EDWARDS AIR FORCE BASE, CALIFORNIA – 1983

The Decider

It's not easy being "The Decider" – but someone must make the tough calls.

Few would ever attempt to glamorize the job of program manager, least of all me. I've spent more of my career in this role in various companies than I cared to, finding the job interesting due to its focus on people and team-building. Scope, schedule, budget, risks and mitigations – interesting at times, never glamorous.

The stakes were seldom high enough – a delayed deliverable and an uncomfortable call to a disappointed customer – ho hum.

But early in my career I was blessed with witnessing a program manager do something so amazing, to me at least, that some glitz did rub off and attach itself to this otherwise mundane role.

And that was the day I witnessed *the decider*.

It was a cold morning in the high desert of California, Edwards Air Force Base, legendary home of the country's greatest test pilots and most audacious aircraft and space vehicles. As a newly-minted employee of Rockwell International, my dream of working the space program was in sight. But for now, instead, I worked on our nation's defense, in the form of the B-1B Strategic Bomber.

The flawed application of resources to this project was no secret. I was very aware even then that the B-1B was merely a dusting off of the earlier B-1A that President Carter had correctly killed and that Reagan had reinstated. History credits Reagan with "winning" the Cold War, but it would be foolish to argue that the B-1B had any hand in the outcome, aside from being a symbolic demonstration that the new president would go to any expense, fund any outmoded weapons system, to push the Soviet Union into collapse.

In the mid-1970s the low-flying, terrain-hugging B-1A was supposed to replace the canceled high altitude B-70 Valkyrie. As early as the downing of Francis Gary Powers, Soviet missiles proved the fallacy of the B-70 strategy, and after it killed several pilots, the program was canceled.

In contrast, the B-1A would fly low and slow over enemy territory, hugging the terrain and evading both radar and missiles. The precise solution that intelligent cruise missiles introduced at the same time. Like the Valkyrie, the B-1B was white-boarded at least five years too late.

I knew that. Many of my senior colleagues, some of them World War II veterans, spoke openly on this, but pointed out that when the nation calls you to do a job, you do it. My boss, himself a B-17 pilot who'd survived bailing out of his plane and two years in a German POW camp – had suggested my counterparts and I drive up to Edwards to experience firsthand the B-1B's maiden flight.

We arrived at the base just after dawn. Our employee badges saw us swiftly whisked through the gate and into an immense hangar where two more of the swept-wing bombers were in final stages of integration.

We viewed them from an elevated position two stories above the hangar floor, through angled glass like that of an airport control tower. A uniformed colonel was hovering over a row of equipment manned by uniformed men and women. The glasses on his face played with the bright light of the monitors below. The scene reminded me of the bridge of an Imperial Cruiser in Empire Strikes Back.

We didn't stay long and hurried out to the action. The third fuselage at Edwards was a fully operational B-1B bomber – or at least, that was the measure of what would be tested today.

Military personnel in camouflage with pant legs tucked neatly into their boots and technicians mostly in white swarmed about the plane. It was a long, needle-nosed bullet, its wings each burdened with dual-exhaust jet engines that emitted roiling and bubbling optical gremlins of heated air.

We strolled forward to join a line of 30 or so spectators and officials, most of whom clearly had some kind of function. While my friends and I worked on the avionics test software, we had no specific mission, we were mere observers. Sensitive to that reality, I double-checked my badge and clearance were visible hanging from the lapel of my vintage flight jacket. I noticed a tall man in a business suit – civilian, with a Rockwell badge like mine: the program flight director. He glanced in our direction before returning his gaze to the aircraft. It seemed our presence would not be questioned.

The engines were howling yet we were close enough to the director to hear him shout to a camouflaged man with a clipboard, "Final checklist."

The camo man shook his head slightly, turned and ran under the aircraft fuselage to a ladder. As he grabbed the rungs he dropped the clipboard, but it merely drifted to his side, held round his neck by a lanyard. He swiftly ascended and disappeared inside.

A few seconds later we could see his blond hair through the canopy, alongside the pilots. He was gesturing at his clipboard and communicating with the flight crew, who remained fixed on their instruments. One of the pilots swiveled in his chair and seemed to point at the checklist. The camo man shook his head vigorously, and disappeared.

He came back down the ladder, and stepped briskly to the program director. He gestured with his pen at the clipboard. The director stood impassive and unmoving, arms crossed over his chest.

It was difficult to hear, but it was obvious what the camo man's message was: we've got a problem, we can't fly right now. His pen jabbed at the clipboard for emphasis. He seemed very emphatic.

The program director was unmoved. He stood still, his coat swaying in the morning breeze, sunglasses leveled over the camo-man's head at the cockpit. The camo man continued his tirade. He turned and pointed toward the engine on the starboard wing while continuing his argument.

The program director said nothing as the camo-man halted his diatribe, and looked up expectantly for some kind of decision.

The program director, arms still crossed, lifted his right thumb. He wanted this bird to fly.

In the canopy, there was motion. The two pilots were suddenly both animated, their helmeted heads bobbing and swiveling. After a few seconds, a gloved thumbs up became visible from one of the pilots.

The program director put a hand on the shoulder of the camo-man. This time, we could hear the words, just barely. "Let's fly."

The camo man did not agree. He flung his head back at the pilots, jabbed his pen once again at the clipboard and then turned back to the program director. This time, his words too were clear.

"Sir, we've got an issue. We cannot fly."

To which the program director merely nodded, and re-asserted a thumbs up to the pilot, who promptly returned the gesture.

The remainder of the camo-man's objections were not audible as the engines began to race and a steady thunder intervened to render all unintelligible. Suffice to say that the camo-man was not actually giving up, but at last, he held both hands up just above shoulder level, and stood aside, next to the program director.

All of us present knew that just months prior a modified B-1A had taken off here and shortly after stalled. The plane had pancaked into the desert floor, but not before the crew escape module had detached. Its chutes barely had time to inflate before it, too, slammed into the desert. Over the company radio link, we'd heard the fateful report real-time. "Three crew Charlie. One Echo." Charlie meant that the three were conscious. Echo meant that the fourth man had expired – killed on impact.

A warm tempest engulfed us as the plane rolled. The engines surged, the aircraft leapt forward. It lifted into the air, and glided upward ever so gently – as if the pilots themselves had agreed with the camo man – until nearly disappearing. It roared back over the base and accelerated loudly at low altitude.

An hour later, it set down gently amid puffs of dust on the dry lake bed. A successful first flight.

Over the next few years 100 of these planes would be built and flown, and a few did crash. More pilots died. The Cold War ended and the mission of the B-1B was undone, a victim of cost, impracticality, obsolescence, and having been superseded by superior technology – most particularly, stealth.

The lesson I learned was clear: decisions must be made, consequences born, and someone has got to assume responsibility. There's no glory to be had, but plenty of responsibility to bear when things go wrong.

You really have to want to be the decider.

First flight of the B-1B Strategic Bomber

EDWARDS AIR FORCE BASE, CALIFORNIA – 1982

Combat Vision

*When thousands stare into empty sky and you're the first fool
to start yelling, you may have combat vision.*

The NASA press pass I'd acquired for the first
launch of the Space Shuttle got me a lot of leverage. I
automatically received press passes for the next few
launches and landings, as if I'd been inducted into the
NASA event-of-the-month club.

They were building a big runway for the Shuttle
landings in Florida, to get the orbiter back where it
belonged more expeditiously. Only a few more
would land in my backyard, at Edwards Air Force
base in the high desert of southern California – just a
few hour's drive for me. I was determined to attend
the 5ᵗʰ and final landing planned for the west coast. I
received the pass in the mail.

My friend, Rob, was interested. Word spread,
and suddenly six people wanted to go. Rob's car
wasn't up to the task. "We'll take Pru's VW bus,"
suggested another friend. "We'll need to rendezvous
in Lancaster, since she's going to visit her mom in

Bishop after the landing."

If you remember the U2 album "The Joshua Tree" and a song called "Where the Streets Have No Name," I'm pretty darn sure they were singing about Lancaster. It's the kind of town where tumbleweeds roll down the streets; and no, the streets do not have names, just letters and numbers: A Street, 5th Street…

The rendezvous went without a hitch.

"You got the pass?" asked Pru.

As if I were going to forget. "Here we go," I said, placed it on her dashboard, and clambered into the back. The pass got us waved through the security entrance at Edwards. We were rolling toward the most storied dry lake bed in aviation history. It was the proving ground of the X-15 and Northrop's Flying Wing. It was also where supersonic travel started with Chuck Yeager's run in the Bell X-1. Come to think of it, it was the test ground for the U-2 spy plane that inspired the Irish rock band. A copycat Irish band named itself Bell X-1. It's all a bit incestuous, if you overthink it.

Not every moment at Edwards was so proud. Before it was named for Edwards, a fallen World War II test pilot, it had been Muroc Proving Ground. Among the experiments conducted at Muroc in an effort to win the war, was the arming of bats.

The whole "Batman" mythos has far more basis in reality than many know. Bats were known to have extraordinary powers of navigation. At some point, an Army Air Corp "brainiac" who should remain unnamed formulated the idea of strapping incendiary explosives onto thousands of bats, who could then be dropped from high-flying B-29 aircraft over Japanese cities. The bats would home in on the bright lights that attracted the most insects, and was where people were sheltering. The incendiaries would detonate, setting vast portions of any targeted city aflame.

This harebrained scheme was actually tested at Muroc. The bats proved too independent to fly en masse toward the intended targets. As a result, most of the air base was burned to the ground. The bat soldier martyrdom was not totally in vain, as the disaster resulted in the immediate cancellation of the whole fire-bat program. Shortly after the war ended, Chuck Yeager broke the sound barrier at Muroc, and its reputation was forever redeemed.

We joined thousands of eager viewers for the shuttle landing, which would happen at 6:33am, give or take a few seconds. Such is the certainty of orbital mechanics. The Shuttle is a huge glider, and the astronaut pilots get only one shot at the runway.

Just a few moments before landing, the crowd grew very quiet. All eyes were straining into the cobalt blue morning sky, looking for the tell-tale sign of a spaceship returning to Earth.

I'm color-blind. For some reason, though, I have what many have called extraordinary night vision. They are supposed to be related phenomena. My night vision is so good that nobody wanted to play hide and seek with me at night when we were kids. It was just too easy for me to spot the hiders.

As I surveyed the canopy above, I remembered what Chuck Yeager had described as "Combat Vision." Flying piston-driven mustangs over Europe in World War II, Yeager and his fellow pilots worked to adjust their focus, from far away, to really far away, to infinity. It was how the sharp-eyed fliers spotted enemy planes long before they themselves were noticed by the enemy.

I practiced my combat vision. The desert was nearly silent, just a rustle of wind through the Joshua trees and parked campers. Then I saw it.

The black diamond of the Shuttle's delta wing, far above the dry lake bed. "There!" I shouted, pointing. "There!"

"Where?"

Va-boom!! Va-boom!! The Shuttle's signature double sonic booms rocked everything for miles around. More silence. Most people still didn't see it. Then slowly, the cheering began. Hitting denser and wetter air, the black diamond began to leave a white contrail as it circled back toward the runway. The crowd noise built to an eerie din as the Shuttle leveled-out and slowly descended toward the lake bed.

Its wheels seemed to hang above it forever before gently touching, sending plumes of dust into the air. Slowly, the front landing gear also drifted down and contacted the earth. The vehicle seemed to roll forever; in fact, the crew were applying "max brake" with no parachutes to test how quickly it could stop on its own. It did finally halt, a magnificent machine alone in the middle of a vast dusty desert.

"Unbelievable," said Rob.

"Amazing," I agreed. We walked back to the VW Bus, which was no longer where it had been parked. "They must have driven over to the reception site," I said.

"Without us?"

It was two miles away, so we figured we'd hang out and tour some nearby static aircraft displays. Two hours later, the VW bus reappeared. "Oh, there you guys are, get the hell in!"

"What's the rush?" I asked.

"We need to get to Bishop and you're slowing us down." We jumped in. They told us all about meeting the astronauts and blah blah. When we got to Lancaster, Pru said, "Get out fast! We're late."

"No worries," I said, grabbing my NASA pass off her dash. There was some satisfaction watching her cringe as the valued keepsake departed from the vehicle and escaped her clutches.

While it would have been nice to meet the astronauts, the events of the day were too monumental to trouble ourselves over the company that had brought us all there. A spaceship had landed on Earth, and I'd seen it first, thanks to Chuck Yeager combat vision training.

TAIWAN – 1987

Belligerence

Leave your preconceived notions in your home country.

The car hurtled down the street at us, seemingly out of nowhere. Hailing from pedestrian-friendly California and already halfway across the narrow back-alley street, Jake and I continued forward, with a bit more spring in our step, but not enough.

It was early morning. We'd just left our apartment of several months in a small city in Taiwan, and were on our way to grab a traditional Taiwanese breakfast – a greasy fried dough stick and a bowl of hot soy milk.

Cheap and remarkably tasty, it had become a part of our comfortable morning ritual. We'd wake, put on shorts and t-shirts, cross the street, have a quick hot breakfast, and return to shower and shave before starting the day. Normally, that meant teaching English as a second language to the very eager students of The Republic of China.

There was something about the rules of the road that we didn't understand. New Yorkers understand it, though differently. Californians, however, are truly spoiled pedestrian brats. We expect vehicular traffic to make the extra effort required to spare the lives of errant pedestrians. We now learned that the rules were different in Taiwan.

Even as we accelerated across the street, the driver of the only vehicle on that calm morning street accelerated, too. He saw we intended to cross, and that we had no intention of backing off and seeking refuge on the sidewalk we'd just departed.

The car was moving at nearly 50 miles per hour as it angled into the oncoming lane to cut off our rapid advance to the opposing sidewalk. Jake and I realized at the last second that the race was going to be a draw; that is, we were about to die. With no choice but suicide remaining, we both halted in our tracks. We were hardly two meters from the refuge we'd sought on the opposing sidewalk.

The driver continued to accelerate and threaded the eye of the needle. He barely missed the curb, and I had to look down to see if my toes were going to be run over. I was in shock that we were suddenly so close to being flattened.

As the car sped past inches away, I lashed out. I swept the back of my hand on the rear side fender. It hurt, and it made a fairly loud "thwack!" My knuckles stung from the impact.

A screech of brakes and clouds of burning rubber ensued. The car came to a complete halt within seconds. Jake and I continued to stand where we'd been forced to pause, as the driver threw it into reverse and barreled back toward us.

He stopped the car, again inches from us, and leapt out of his vehicle. He was dressed in a bright yellow short-sleeve shirt, slacks, and black shoes. He came around the car, his finger pointing accusingly, and began to yell at us in angry, salty Chinese.

Jake is a big guy. He's six foot two and built like the Special Forces Ranger he is. The little yellow-shirted man did not hesitate at this. He seemed to think Jake had attacked his car.

I'm not a big guy. I was about the same height as the driver. I straightened him out. "Hey, I hit your car. I'll do it again now if you don't move it. We're trying to cross the street. You're in our way."

His finger was hitting my chest. I returned the favor, which he really didn't seem to like.

It was clear to Jake what was happening here. Plus, his Chinese is pretty good. "You!" he shouted at me for the driver's enjoyment. "You don't hit people's cars!" The driver was looking smug and puffed his chest out.

"And you," Jake said, poking the poor fellow in the chest, "You don't poke your finger like this at another person." The driver flinched away and cussed. He kept up a stream of complaints but he retreated to the driver's side of his vehicle. Still cursing, he jumped in and screeched away.

"What we have here," said Jake, "is a classic clash of cultures. Cars rule in Taiwan."

"He nearly killed us," I pointed out.

"That's why he's so mad," said Jake. "He spared our lives, then we went and HIT his car."

A long time later, when I wasn't so pissed off, I finally saw the poor driver's logic. He had spared us.

So, if you're out there, sorry about that. And thanks, buddy!

TAIWAN – 1987

The Sentinels

Appearances are ever deceptive.

"We'll swing by the office first," said Stan, who drove the manic streets of Taiwan like a native. He'd actually learned to drive, like many Latter Day Saints, on the quiet streets of Provo, Utah. "Which means we can swing by something you'll find interesting."

"The Chiang Kai-Shek Memorial?" I said. "I've already seen it."

"The Temporary Resting Place. No, this one's off the beaten path."

"You're kidding, right?" The Chiang Kai-Shek Memorial Hall is a gargantuan monument comprised of millions of tons of masonry on a majestic scale. It is a modern day pyramid for the man who'd saved the Republic of China by moving its seat of government from mainland China to Taiwan 'temporarily' when Mao's forces had finally won the revolution that ended in 1949. "Nobody really expects Chiang's final resting place will eventually return to the mainland, do they?"

"Quite a few still do," assured Stan. "It's more than just a dream for them, especially the old-timers who barely escaped the clutches of the People's Republic. You know the Nationalists maintained a standing army in the forests of northern Thailand until just a decade ago. Ten to twenty thousand troops formed the nucleus of the reinvasion force, a persistent thorn in Mao's side."

"Come on," I said. "If the U.S. didn't support that during the peak of the cold war, we're sure not going to now." It was 1987. The Berlin Wall had not yet crumbled, but the trend lines were clear.

"Maybe not," said Stan, "but don't try to tell that to the old guard." He downshifted hard into second gear as the car raced up a steep and narrow incline. Atop the hill was a large house, surrounded by a tall, wrought iron fence. The engine whine tapped out as we crested the rise, and Stan stopped across the street from the house.

Unlike the "Temporary Resting Place" there was nothing particularly grand about it. It was simple, with a large green lawn, something almost unseen in Taiwan, and a clear sign of importance and wealth. Aside from a nice but unremarkable view of Taipei sprawl and the lawn, the house could be any of the well-to-do large homes in this district of Taipei.

In fact, the neighborhood didn't seem particularly savory, what with several idle teenagers loitering nearby. I spotted three right away, then a fourth. They were hanging out on the sidewalk near the house and across the street. Two of them were giving us and our car quite the glare.

"Are those gang members?" I asked.

"The kids? Oh no, no, not at all." Stan

informed me. "Not in the least. Although, in a way, it depends on your perspective."

The one closest to us wore a white t-shirt and Levi's jeans. Over his shoulder was a black belt that held a leather pouch by his right hip.

All the teenagers wore the same kind of pouch.

"That's the presidential residence," said Stan, pointing to the house.

"That's Taiwan's equivalent of 10 Downing Street?"

"Good way to put it. Yes."

"Then why do they let these gang kids hang out?" I asked.

"Well, you know what's in those pouches?"

"Drugs?"

"No. Those are 45 magnums, and the kids know how to shoot."

The presidential detail. These were the "less conspicuous" of the sentinels defending Taiwan's leader.

"Wow," I said. "No wonder they're giving us the eye."

"Can never be too careful when guarding the leadership," said Stan. "Especially when two foreigners roll up in a jalopy."

He waved at the nearest kid and started to roll us back down the hill. I watched the kid's eyes. He was deadly serious, and his hand was right on that pouch button. Best not to mess with these sentinels.

MALAYSIA – 1987

Train to Hell

Train hard, travel easy. Maybe the other way around.

The next destination for Jake and me: Kuala Lumpur, Malaysia. The train was the logical way to get there from peninsular Thailand, after a grueling bus ride from Bangkok south. The train! It sounded like sheer bliss.

And so it began. The train trundled out of the Hat Yai station on a warm afternoon. It wouldn't arrive in KL until nearly midnight as it made many stops. We traveled through dense forests with few visible inhabitants to the soundtrack of an awesome drone of unseen insects. One could only imagine the number and size of the critters that could generate so many decibels.

The arachnid empire, on the other hand, was very visible. Like almost all railways in the world, this one was paralleled with communications and power poles that ran the length to KL. Between the multiple lines of the power cables were spider webs. In most places, these webs were highlighted by concentrated quantities of the most massive spiders I have ever seen. Their bodies appeared to be the size of my fist. These were meaty creatures who were clearly congregated not merely out of the social imperative of each other's company, but rather because here was food aplenty.

Soon food appeared on our slow train. After about the fifth or sixth jungle station and thereafter at nearly every station, as the train lurched to a halt, we heard the cries of the vendors as they boarded, dashed up and down the entire train once, and then leapt off as the train began to roll. Their cries were loud and clear, and always the same.

"One chicken, one dollar! Two chicken, two dollar!"

These full-service food providers even did the math for you. It was a nice touch. The first time they rushed through our car, Jake and I found ourselves reaching for Malaysian dollars in the pockets of our shorts. That is, until we got a good look at the chicken.

We came to call them "chicken-on-a-stick" since each piece of meat was framed by a sort of popsicle stick crucifix. We saw no chicken meat there. Any lawyer worth their salt would have corrected the vendors: "That is not chicken on a stick. Why, let it be known from here to the ends of the Earth, that is, in fact, lizard-on-a-stick!"

It was, admittedly, lizard tastefully arranged on a popsicle crucifix. It just wasn't our thing.

Which is why, shortly after nightfall when the train made a protracted "dinner stop" at an isolated village with a single restaurant, Jake and I ordered up and dug in. The food was simple, different from the

Thai fare we'd been enjoying for weeks, spicy, hot, and tasty. It was all good.

Except for the bacterial part that wasn't. Somehow, something survived all that heat and spice and went to work on our guts. By the time the train arrived in KL at nearly midnight, we weren't feeling so hot. By the next morning, we were sick at a level I'm not sure we even understood.

For two days, we hardly left our hotel room, and only then to fetch Coca-Cola or some other well-branded bottled beverage from the hotel gift shop. Our main activities those two days involved very frequent visits to the toilet. In my delirium, I decided my next great invention would be the dual-use toilet: one that enables simultaneous emissions from both the entry and exit digestive portals, if you catch my drift. We could have really used that.

Late on the afternoon of the third day, it was as if Jake and I woke for the first time. "Did we eat anything recently?" he asked.

No, we had not.

"I'm not ready for any more Malaysian cuisine," I pointed out.

"No problem," said Jake. "Let's go to A&W." He'd been looking at it out our window for the past 72 hours, and now it all made sense. "It's right there, and it should be like any A&W Root Beer in the world," he added optimistically; we knew there was a chance it was a knock-off, but desperate times require desperate measures.

We gingerly stepped the 100 meters or so to the A&W and then — seeing no lizard on the menu -- ordered burgers and root beer. Then a second round. It was ambrosia. With the return of hunger the bad bacteria were gone.

Our faculties now in recovery mode, we reflected. I asked: "Why didn't we try the chicken-on-a-stick? It probably would have saved us a lot of misery."

Very likely true. If it wasn't Shakespeare who said this, it should have been. "Fear not the chicken in lizard's clothing. Fear only the chicken half-baked."

LAS VEGAS – 1989

Gaming the System

Planning is important. It's nothing without execution.

Shortly after the dawn of the personal computer revolution, opportunity beckoned. Some people wrote software and sold it over retail counters. Others launched services that harnessed the databasing and processing power of the PC to help people find a job, a date, or other people with the same interests.

I put my own Atari 800 computer to work simulating roulette.

In high school, I'd had some programming classes under the tutelage of Alan B. Crokemall. He was one of those rare high school teachers in the late 1970s who maintained absolute decorum – three piece suit, starched shirt, striped tie. His one concession to the changing times was a full but neat beard that must have been trimmed on a daily basis.

Precision is exactly what computers demand, and Crokemall was as precise as precision gets in human form. One assignment he gave me, tailored to my slow learning curve, was to write a program that found the sum of all prime numbers between zero and 1,000. It was not difficult, but I struggled with it. My subroutine divided each number by all preceding positive integers, looking for the presence, absence, and quality of any remainder. Then it added one and repeated the process.

At long last, I'd debugged the final error, prepared a new set of punch cards, and ran them through the card reader, which went "ka-chunk, ka-chunk" as it digested each card.

Excited to see a string of prime numbers emerge onto the dot matrix printer, I manually calculated the first 20 primes, and the lists matched. I had it. The project wasn't due for a few hours, so I cracked open my latest science fiction read, *Dune*, and put my feet up.

The next day, Mr. Crokemall handed back our graded assignments. "Overall good work, folks. To the extent that you followed instructions, you did great." I couldn't help but notice his gaze at me upon that last phrase. Oh, crap.

"An 'A' for Mr. Ross, there you are," he said handing the printout back to my friend. "An 'A' for Mr. Flagels, well done. And Jenkins, here is your B minus."

"What?" I mumbled.

"Good job finding all the primes, that was the hard part. Unfortunately, you skipped the easy part, which was adding them up."

I slapped my forehead. It was a lesson I would not soon forget. Always solve the problem, the whole problem, and nothing but the problem.

So now with the far greater processing power of my own personal computer, I knew that checking and double-checking both the results AND the objective, as well as the inputs into the results, were all critical.

I had already mastered certain frowned upon techniques and was doing very well at the blackjack tables on my visits to Las Vegas (as exemplified in my previous story "Twenty-One"). Yet I'd been entranced watching my friend Roger play roulette. He seemed to have amazingly good luck in a game that was of course tuned to be entirely in the casino's favor. I was quite sure if I played the results would not be as good.

There was another aspect to roulette that intrigued me. It applied, I knew, to all forms of wagering, yet seemed to be more readily applied to this particular game. If you kept increasing your bet every time you lost a spin of the wheel, eventually your number would come up. The question was, would you earn back all the money you'd previously lost and make a profit?

Yes. That is, you would if you did not first run into the table limit. The table limit existed for two very good reasons: to mitigate the total risk to the house of any particular bet; and to ensure nobody got away with betting increasing wagers until at last the law of averages gave them a win – and a guaranteed profit. How to get there without hitting the max bet?

That's what I set out to simulate on my Atari computer. I wrote a little routine that quickly showed that, win or lose, I'd very soon be betting rather extraordinary sums of money, with strong probability of being foiled by the table limit. However, there might be another way.

Instead of doubling the wager after each loss, using a smaller multiplier would reduce the total amount at risk. Further, there were bets that would win more often, with lower payback, of course, such that the maximum bet wouldn't get too crazy.

After a long time of playing around with the rules of roulette and running simulations, I narrowed in on what seemed like a winning formula. About 85% of the time, a cycle of wagering would result in winnings for the player.

The formula began with a $1 wager placed at the corner of four numbers. This allowed for payout of 8-to-1 if any of the four numbers hit. The betting increment was optimized at 1.28 times the previous bet. Of course, betting $1 followed by $1.28 would be impractical if not a violation of the house rules. However, with rounding, I could achieve the multiple of 1.28 on an average basis with approximately the same results.

For example, the first and second bets would be $1. The third and fourth bets would be $2. The fifth bet would be $3 and the sixth bet $4. From there, the rounding became less statistically important.

In a nutshell, I would bet 'four corners' with a payout of 8-to-1. I would increase the wager increment by a rounded 128% after each loss. With a cap below the $200 maximum bet I could lose up to 14 times in a row before the cycle ended. The chances of winning one of the bets was better than 85%. If after 14 spins and losses – which should happen about 15% of the cycles – I would reset the wager to $1 and begin a new cycle.

The program showed this to be a winning strategy, if perfectly executed. Over many cycles, the pot of winnings grew. It was a jagged growth with many highs and lows, but the sawtooth was not defeating the trend-line, and that's all that counted.

I prepared a cheat-sheet to give the precise bets for each round so I wouldn't have to calculate on the spot. The system would require at least two people: one would place wagers on the table and the other would instruct and guide the activity. So much coordination between two people at the roulette table could not be hidden from the pit boss or dealer. They would have to agree to let us try out our little system.

"Systems" were what ignorant tourists tried out with great regularity, and casinos love them. The existence of a system virtually guarantees more winnings for the house as nearly all fail.

Roger and I walked into the Stardust casino in Las Vegas. We took $800 cash to the gaming table. We put the first $200 on the felt and got the dealer's attention.

"Can we get," I glanced down at my cheat-sheet, "Forty singles and the rest in fives?"

The dealer nodded and started doling out chips. The stacks of chips attracted the attention of the pit boss. He walked over to observe the commotion. "What you got there?" he asked, glancing at the notepad in my hand.

"We've got a system we want to try out."

"You've got a system for winning roulette?" he laughed. "Have fun, knock yourselves out."

Six other players were putting their money onto the felt. Roger placed a dollar on the corner of four numbers. The dealer fired the ball into what I call 'the centrifuge' where it whirled in countersink to the spin of the wheel. About ten seconds later he said, "final bets" and held his hand out in a 'stop' motion.

The little white ball slowed then gently fell into the spinning wheel where it bounced crazily before settling into the groove of number 11. It was a loss, and not just for us. One player had bet a dollar on black, and 11 being black, he retrieved his one dollar winnings. The dealer swept away all the other chips from the felt and betting began again.

Roger placed a dollar for the second bet. Same result. We upped the bet to two dollars per the cheatsheet. The pit boss followed our antics with amusement.

On the eighth spin, we won. The payout put us $12 ahead. The pit boss shrugged and walked over to view the blackjack tables.

On the next cycle, we went 14 spins without winning. That was supposed to happen only once in six cycles, so it hurt. No problem, though. Statistically, it was bound to happen sometimes. I put down two more $100 bills and specified the same set of chips.

A win on the fourth spin, very early, added back only $6. We were now down about $180, but the next cycle we won on the twelfth spin. With each new cycle I flipped to a fresh sheet, and made sure Roger's chip stacking was ready to load the felt per our formula. It was mechanically more demanding than I'd expected.

We won the next three cycles and had regained much of our losses, nearly back to scratch. The pit boss wandered back and asked, "How you scammers doing?"

Shoulder shrug. We counted at blackjack in camouflage; being out in the open was a bit strange.

We won the next cycle after seven spins. The pit

boss looked a little more interested now.

Then something went wrong. We lost 13 spins of the cycle, and with the final spin remaining were having trouble getting the right combination of chips out onto the felt in time. Something wasn't feeling right as Roger shoved the pile of chips out onto our four numbers. I began counting what was laid out….ten dollars short!

Yet we won. The dealer placed the winning marker on top of one of our four numbers. The pit boss did not look pleased, and gave me a scowl. It was unnerving. We'd won at the most opportune time, the 14th spin, yet our betting error cost us $80 in winnings. Painful.

The next cycle began. We went 14 spins without a win. I suggested to Roger that we re-group.

We cashed out our chips and retreated to the casino café and ordered some drinks. "Ok, what have we got…"

We were down $90, almost the exact amount we'd failed to win due to money management issues. We decided to re-caffeinate, re-group, and re-trench.

We went back to the table and proceeded to lose the very next cycle. One time in six? We were now down $270 and were not feeling too swell.

"Try one more, or let's go play blackjack?" asked Roger.

I made the call. I wasn't happy about it. I knew we could do it, but on the other hand 21 was just so much easier. "Blackjack. We'll try this again later if we pile up some reserves."

On that particular trip, while we won back some money, we didn't quite feel like the buffer was big enough. So, no more roulette. On the next trip, we just didn't have the gumption. Blackjack was way more fun.

The Pit Boss – aka Mr. Big -- could breathe a sigh of relief. The best laid plans of computers and men had come to naught, a victim of complex execution.

Never dress like this in a real casino

BANGKOK, THAILAND – 1989

Hot Pursuit

Your future mother-in-law would not approve.

Halfway through the four-year overseas courtship that resolved with marriage to the woman of my pursuit, an opportunity presented itself. "My mom and I will be in a tour group in December," Shelly had informed me. "We'll go to Hong Kong, Thailand, and Malaysia. Maybe you can meet us there."

I did just that. Shelly and her mother flew from Taiwan, while I flew from Los Angeles. Our plan was to meet in the lobby of the hotel where her large Taiwanese tour group was staying in Bangkok, which she informed me was named "The NASA Garden Hotel."

"Can you spell it?" I asked her. "It sounded like you said 'NASA'." She spelled it out. It was NASA. I was intrigued, and immediately tried to book a room there too.

"All sold," said the hotel clerk. "Big tour group from Taiwan." Shelly's tour group comprised of six fully-loaded buses of tourists from her homeland. I had to make alternate arrangements.

The problem was that there were very few other hotels in that remote section of Bangkok. I zeroed in on the closest, which was still nearly a mile away. It was called "The Secret Inn" and was affordable. With dusk descending, I flagged a cab and showed him the address that a helpful friend on Kho San Road had scrawled for me. Kho San Road is the official foreign ghetto for backpackers visiting Thailand from around the world.

"You go here?"

"Yes," I confirmed.

"You go here, alone?"

"Yes, no other passengers." I was thinking maybe this particular taxi company charged by the head. He looked a little confused.

"Alone? No girl?"

I reiterated my bachelor status. He shrugged his

shoulders in that universal, 'okay, what the hell' manner that translates across all linguistic boundaries, and charged into the brutal Bangkok traffic.

An hour later, we approached the hotel in the dark. I assumed we were, as he tapped the glass of his window and pointed at a building. "You sure, here?"

Not knowing what he was pointing at, I opted to say "Yes, that's it." Immediately, I worried that I'd made an error. He drove into a dimly lit subterranean garage and made a series of turns between tall imposing cement posts. He pulled up to a dark spot where a uniformed man with a cap promptly jerked the car door open.

"Sawadi kap," the man whispered, and waved me out of the cab with a white-gloved hand holding a red flashlight. He peered into the backseat from which I'd just emerged as I paid the cabbie.

"Alone?" asked the flashlight man. The cabbie explained, yes, alone. I followed the man. He opened a door and waved me in with his light. "You want get girl?"

"No, thanks." The penny was dropping now as I saw the mirrored ceiling and soft pink hues of the round bed, which I quickly discovered was a waterbed. I'd heard about these places. A love hotel. This one specialized in secrecy and security. I suppose maybe they all do.

Notwithstanding, I quickly showered and changed into clean shorts and my only collared shirt.

Then I exited through the same door I'd come in. The only door. Into a very dark garage.

After fumbling about for a time, I chanced into the man with the red flashlight. "What want?" he asked. "Girl?"

"No, no I just want to get out. I need to go to NASA Garden Hotel." He seemed very put out, but eventually led me to the driveway and ushered me into the night air. "Get girl," he said. I expect he had figured out I was going out to get my girlfriend, and he wasn't entirely incorrect.

Using a worn, sweaty map and asking every rare passerby on the street, I eventually found the NASA. It was a five or six story edifice with the 1970s era NASA logo poorly but unmistakably stolen and put in giant letters on its roof.

In the lobby, I was able to dial Shelly's room, and I met her and her mom in the hotel bar for a quick drink. "Sorry," she said, "it's late, so we have to go to sleep."

"No problem," I said.

"Tomorrow, our group goes to Pattaya Beach. Can you meet us there?"

"Sounds great," I said. I'd studied the tour itinerary she'd given me, and had plans to rent a motorbike.

Shelly's mom, a quiet lady with a pleasant smile, asked me a question. "She wants to know where you're staying." I had the answer in my back pocket, and flashed the hotel card. It was then that I realized the card was free of any linguistic ambiguity.

The card face had a big red heart and featured a cartoon doughy-eyed young woman with a crimson lip-stick smile. It was, shall we say, an awkward moment. To her immense credit, Shelly barked a few words of explanation to her mother, whose own eyes had gone wide. Mom recovered and smiled at me.

"My mom thinks you should look for a better

hotel, like this one," she said. I couldn't have agreed more. I'd always wanted to join NASA.

The next day I zoomed down the byways on my rented motorbike, and again caught up with Shelly and her mom, this time at Pattaya Beach. I had moved to a humble, ramshackle room not far from their hotel. When I couldn't produce sufficient cash in the right denominations to pay for it, a young woman gave me a 100 Baht bill. "Pay me back later," she said. I would have, but never saw her again.

That was the afternoon of 31 December 1989, New Year's Eve, and the end of a decade. I met Shelly and invited her to stroll on the beach.

That was when I noticed the ship.

PATTAYA BEACH, THAILAND – 1989

The Final Voyage

There are no dumb questions. Or at most, one.

Shelly later told me that she thought we were both going to die and, if we didn't, she would certainly be done with me. It turns out, she was wrong on both counts.

We'd strolled on the warm sands in the late afternoon and I could not keep my eyes off that ship. Yes, I was enjoying the company, and we even held hands a bit here and there. Our two-year long friendship was maybe, just now, turning into something else. Still, that ship was a hauntingly familiar phantom. Perhaps five kilometers offshore, it was an immense gray ghost dominating the sea between the beach and the horizon.

Some things I knew for a fact: it was an American warship, and it was no cruiser. It was a full-blown battleship, with multiple huge gun turrets. When we came upon a jet-ski rental, I asked her casually, "Care to ride out a bit on one of these?"

"Sure," she said, probably just to be polite. The term "wine-dark sea" has never applied more in my reckoning than it did as we plowed into the chop of the Gulf of Siam. The rental included one life jacket, which I had Shelly wear. I assumed this would give her a sense of safety and confidence.

The immense distance was a challenge. Before long, I realized we'd never get there unless I put the spurs to this ride, and I throttled up. The wind, the spray, the bounce across the waves, all felt right. The further we got from shore, the more she was glancing back at me.

"Are you okay?" I asked her. She said nothing, so I throttled back. We were almost there and it was a warship, after all. The crew would not take kindly to our racing up on it.

"We're really far from shore," Shelly said. "And I'm not a good swimmer."

I reassured her that the jet-ski and her lifejacket were not going to sink. It seemed to help.

Our more gentle approach gave me a chance to study the looming ship. It was an immensely tall, steel escarpment. The ship was unquestionably either the U.S.S. Missouri or the U.S.S. New Jersey. Ronald Reagan had re-commissioned these two World War II veterans shortly after he'd assumed office in 1981. He'd brought back a lot of aging weapons systems, with updates of course, including a revitalized B-52 bomber and the B-1B, which I'd worked on at Rockwell as my first real job out of college.

A few hundred meters from the hull of the mighty vessel, we slowed to a crawl. I could now see sailors on deck. Some of them were on duty, watching us with binoculars while leaning on a fearsome looking deck gun – one of those dual purpose machine guns that could claw a close-passing aircraft out of the sky, or make mincemeat out of a small vessel -- to say nothing of a Ski-Doo.

The gun wasn't pointed anywhere near us, but I gave a big friendly two-handed wave nonetheless. The sailor with the field glasses waved back. I was going to try to shout some kind of greeting, but the sudden noise of a boat motor gave me pause.

Around the bow of the big ship emerged a launch with a dozen or so sailors in dress uniform gripping a rope rail. The launch pilot was clearly headed to shore, but when he saw our little craft bobbing nearby, he steered toward us. I waved.

"Ahoy," he shouted, slowing 10 meters from us.

"Ahoy!" I responded. "Going ashore?"

One of the other sailors replied with a southern drawl. "Are you American? What the—what are you doing here?"

"I'm from California," I said, "and she is from Taiwan. We're on vacation."

There were big grins on that little launch. "Well, I'll be…! I'm from Alabama. What's Thailand like?"

"It's wonderful, the people are friendly, the food is fantastic. How long are you here?"

The sailor shrugged his shoulders. "Tonight, at least." Ah, shore leave! On New Year's Eve at the end of the decade.

"You'll love it. Where you all headed next?"

A whole lot of smiles. Not a word. Our troops are the best.

I wanted to punch myself. What a stupid question to ask. "Oh, we'll probably steer this $2 billion war machine directly to Singapore for a few days, so now you know where to find it and plant mines to sink it." I suddenly felt not just small but microscopic in the shadow of this goliath. The sailors were obviously cool with the whole thing. They'd had "Loose Lips Sink Ships" ingrained into everything they did.

"Hey, maybe we'll see you onshore!" One of them shouted.

"If so, I'll buy a round. Happy new year!" They hooted and waved as the pilot burped his motor and the launch scudded toward the distant land.

Which reminded me. "Still okay?" I asked Shelly.

"I'm fine. Can we go back now?"

"Your wish is my command." We cruised back in the wake of the launch, but at low speed, taking our time, and minimizing the bounce of wave-action. That night we did not run into the sailors, but we had an incredible New Year's Eve feast with Shelly's tour group leader welcoming me to the outdoor buffet that featured lobster, crab, and Thai curries and delicacies.

It was a magical evening. The battleship offshore fired off a few dozen skyrockets at midnight, which were met with immense joy and excitement by the many partiers onshore.

It's fair to say that it was at that moment when our courtship took a turn from the explorative to the romantic. From that night on it was a matter of when, not if, we'd get married.

And that immense warship? It was, in fact, the U.S.S. New Jersey. Six months later, back in California, I read a newspaper article about its arrival in the states and immediate decommissioning. We had rendezvoused with the great warship on its final voyage. Unless, of course, some future president presses it back into gunboat diplomacy.

GERMAN "CONSULATE" LOS ANGELES – 1990

Kill the Boot!

*Unauthorized extraction of another person's food can have
serious consequences.*

The boot was passed rapidly around the table, bringing a flood of effervescent bubbles and an agreeable German brewery flavor to six thirsty mouths. It was a real glass boot, about knee-high, pure crystal, and at this restaurant it was standard that only one boot be issued at a time to each table. Containing three liters of beer, it tended to pass quickly around the table until drained, at which point a fresh boot would be promptly delivered and the communal consumption continued.

While it was beautiful to look at, all amber and sparkling, the boot was not easy to drink from. First, it stood tall on the table and required two hands. More problematic was its tendency to be tilted in such a manner that a large air bubble would form in the shoe of the boot, and when the quaffer started to lower it back after chugging that air pocket would erupt.

There were six thirsty and hungry folks sitting

around our table at Der Rote Löwe, a two to four time a year tradition for my friends and me. We called it the "German consulate in Los Angeles" due to its utterly authentic German food, beer, atmosphere, and clientele. On occasion we'd spot Japanese tourists at other tables in the dark, cave-like spaces of the restaurant. For the most part, our encounters were with German-speaking customers, and the expat German waitstaff.

The boot, while not particularly sanitary, was an intimate way to share beer with close friends, with whom occasional minor bacterial exchange is probably going to happen in the natural course of events anyway.

Conversation at these dinners was always fluid, and the boot moved round the table with centripetal velocity that typically began slow. It accelerated with the appetizers, went into hyperdrive with the arrival of the main courses – steaming jägerschnitzel mit kartoffel or braunschweiger mit sauerkraut – and slowed and stopped with arrival of coffee and hot apple strudel.

Two refrains were never to be disregarded. The first was, "Pass the boot!" If the person in possession of the boot had clearly taken his or her draught and was now yacking on about something, this was a fit of rudeness that must be called out. The offender would smile and pass the boot (always counterclockwise; I don't know why) and continue yacking.

The second refrain was usually louder, half playful, half serious, and always came as the beer in the boot diminished. The entire table, save the poor fool in possession, would lightly pound the table and repeat. "Kill the boot! Kill the boot!"

Said person would then be obliged to up-end and drain it, thus making way for a freshly filled boot.

Dale was caught with a significant amount, up to the lower end of the heel, and thus the entire foot was nearly flush. "I can't finish all that!" he protested. Nobody believed him. Dale was a legendary eater, notorious for losing his good natured approach to life as his blood sugar dropped. It was the end of a long day sightseeing in L.A. and nearly eight hours since lunch.

"Kill the boot! Kill the boot!" Under such peer pressure, already with a serious beer buzz, and anticipating the arrival at any moment of his entrée, Dale collapsed and entered the challenge with gusto. He lifted the boot, shouted "kill the boot!" and put it to his lips.

He made quick progress, but Dale had made a tactical error. The boot should always be oriented with the toe pointing down or at least to the left or right. Now, as he lifted it higher and guzzled, the toe was pointed to 11 o'clock.

With so much liquid to quaff, he had to pause, and briefly lowered the boot. Suddenly, a flood of liquid amber shot out of the top of the boot, into Dale's nostrils, down the front of his shirt and onto his pants. He nearly drowned, but by golly he killed that boot without flinching and immediately rose. "Gotta wash up after that." The table heartily approved.

The waiter swiftly delivered a fresh boot, this time a slightly darker, heartier brew, better complement to the mountains of food that quickly arrived. In front of Dale's empty seat, he placed a steaming platter of wienerschnitzel mit gravy, topped with two fried eggs.

"Ooh, ahh," someone complemented. There were many admiring eyes; Dale knew how to order. In the seat to the left of Dale's, Cary gazed with longing at the steaming delicacies of Dale's plate. He seemed not to notice his own pig's knuckle.

The boot came to Cary. He paused to begin a tale, caught himself, took a long glug of beer and passed the boot. "That was early in the first semester," he continued, picking up his fork. "All was going well, and little did I know that Dr. Holtz was about to expel me from the class."

Suddenly, without warning, he planted his fork with considerable intensity into one of Dale's eggs, and with a fluid motion it disappeared into his now closed and chewing mouth. "Mmmm," he grunted in primal satisfaction.

It was at that moment, Dale emerged newly freshened from the washroom. He froze as he approached his chair. Tension was high.

"What the....who ate my egg?" Always a quick-study, he picked up on the clues Cary's fork left behind: drops of yolk draped on its tines, more yolk on the cutlet next to the one surviving egg. It was clear the waiter had delivered two eggs, and one had vanished.

Nobody wanted to rat out Cary. Perhaps we should have, that might have spared us all what came next. Cary, among the most honest of human beings, would certainly have come clean but for the fact that he appeared in a daze of utter contentment, the impact of having eaten – apparently – the perfect egg.

"Cary!" cried Dale, and without particular violence, backhanded Cary across the ear. Cary's brown hair was mussed, but he was smiling, looking none the worse for wear.

Dale, having vented his rage, sat down and ate the other egg. The table went back to animated conversation. The boot was quickly drained to be replaced by two more before we throttled back for desert.

As we finished coffee, the incident finally resurfaced when Rich said, "Cary, you can get between Dale and just about anything, but you never want to mess with his food."

Cary handed the boot to Rich. "Amen to that. Now kill the boot!"

The boot went smoothly down.

CORRECT

WRONG – SPLASH DANGER!

Speed Trap

Pulling a fast one on a smart judge is no cakewalk.

"It's an open and shut case," said my roommate, Roger, with a big grin on his face. "I'm off the hook!"

Chris and I were both shaking our heads 'no'. This should have been a tip-off to Roger, but instead he went ahead and asked: "What do you guys think?"

"Review the particulars again," said Chris. "I want to be deadly accurate with my critique and not miss any of the imbecility inherent in your plan."

We could talk this way to each other. You know, friends from high school, still socializing frequently as we approached the grand benchmark of 30. Roger stepped up to the challenge. "What, are you kidding me, Chris? This plan is foolproof."

"Obviously not," I kibitzed. "Because here are two fools who don't think much of your plan."

Roger rose from our living room sofa. "OK, OK, let me lay it out so that even you fools can comprehend the genius of it. My genius!" added Roger, rather unnecessarily, I thought.

He is a very smart guy -- an engineer, a top scholar in high school. He said he didn't so much drop out of Cornell as he decided it was too freaking cold for him in the winters. Still, he had passed Dr. Carl Sagan's astronomy class, which definitely burnished his image in my mind.

To send him off properly for his first Ivy League semester, Chris and I and other friends had driven him to LAX. Then we made a big show of digging for small change we could jam into one of those little flight insurance vending machines. "Hey, buddy," I told him, "we know you're gonna be fine, but if anything *should* happen to your plane, god forbid, and we lost our good friend, we'd at least be able to take some measure of comfort from being millionaires. You get it, right?"

He actually did. In Roger's mind, it all made sense. Almost anything did. That's why I offer the modifier that while Roger is a very smart guy, there are two caveats to his genius. The first and most obvious is that everyone is smart. The lowest IQ human being can still kick butt on the smartest of almost any other species on the planet.

The other caveat, more directly applicable to Roger, is what my older brother famously said about guys like him – and me, which wasn't entirely inaccurate – "All brains and no common sense."

"My car is here." He pointed at the coffee table in our living room, where he had re-built the "scene of the crime" in miniature. He pointed at a white Hot Wheels toy car, a Datsun 240Z. It was Roger's car – all sleek, all engine. "The police car is here." He was talking down to us, which I found amusing. The other Hot Wheels was a black and white police sedan emblazoned with tiny red letters on the doors that said "police." He'd even made a crude mini STOP sign out of popsicle sticks. Even in his late twenties, Roger downed a popsicle or two nearly every night.

"Now, the distance from this stop sign," he pointed carefully, "to where the cop is lying in wait is approximately 38 meters."

"Ahem," voiced Chris. "Did you actually want to win this case? Then you can't be using the metric system and sounding all puffed up about yourself."

"Fine," Roger corrected. "Approximately 120 feet. Now it's well known that the 240Z generates a maximum torque ..."

"Ahem," voiced Chris.

"Fine! Has a maximum zero to 60 *acceleration*," said Roger forcefully, "of eight seconds, powered by 151 horses." Then he lifted his little chalkboard to show us what Newton's equations had to say about all this.

"So, the officer, gentleman that he may be," continued Roger.

"Objection," I stated, "the defense is caricaturing the law enforcement official."

"The *cop*," clarified Roger, "who documented on this ticket," and he then held up the yellow piece of paper in his other hand, "that he clocked me at the intersection, 120 feet away from my cold start, at the speed of 58 miles per hour, was obviously in error. Who you gonna trust? This cop, or Sir Isaac Newton?"

"Objection," I said, "defense is presenting a false dichotomy."

Roger ignored that one. "For the 240Z," he continued, and we knew this would be his closing argument, "amazing sports machine that it is ..."

"Objection," stated Chris, "defense is needlessly embellishing his own image."

Now Roger looked flustered. He paused, and the frustration passed as if it had never been. He finished with a big grin. "It is simply incapable of exceeding 46 miles per hour in the aforementioned distance. From a standing start," he reminded us. It would be a mistake for him to stress this point, as in California very few people make full stops at stop signs. I know Roger didn't.

"Remind us again of the posted speed limit?" I asked.

"That's not the point!" Roger proclaimed. "It was 35. The point is that the cop's documentation is false. When the assertion of law is invalidated by the unerring rule of physics, the data cannot be trusted. The case is open and shut." He sat down, well satisfied with his presentation, and waived the little chalkboard over the Hot Wheels on the coffee table in summation.

"So, NOW what do you think?"

"It's hard to think, honestly," said Chris. "I can only see flames and you going down in them."

"Roger does have a small chance," I offered. "It's called traffic school and the mercy of the courts."

"You'll see," he said. "Open and shut. Let's go eat, I'm famished." We did that.

The following day Roger appeared in traffic court, dressed in his job interview suit which gratuitously included all three pieces. His hair was trim, his glasses freshly cleaned, and he almost looked like a lawyer.

"Next," said the black-robed judge, a rotund man with gray hair that was much too long, swept and brylcreemed straight back. "Roger Padawan vs. Officer Diaz."

Roger bolted up to the defendant's podium.

"Who are you?" asked the judge.

"Your honor," he said respectfully, "I'm Roger Padawan, defendant. If it pleases the court."

The judge suddenly had an itch over his left eyebrow that he vigorously addressed with long fingernails. "State your case, Mr. Pada...Padawama."

"Thank you, your honor." Roger straightened up. He looked like he was about to read the Valedictorian speech at Cornell.

"It's well established that the maximum acceleration—"

"Guilty!" the judge gaveled loudly. "Next!"

My guess is the judge had seen this "defense by law of physics" thing a few times before. We decided to take a little pity on Roger that night, and took him to his favorite restaurant: Kenny Rogers Roasters. Really? Yes. As my older wiser brother always said:

"All brains and no common sense."

OVER THE YELLOW SEA, PACIFIC OCEAN – 1995

Violins In Flight

Best to keep it off the plane.

"Sir," said the flight attendant hovering over my seat, "please give me your passport."

I was mortified by what had just happened aboard the Shanghai to Los Angeles flight.

"Don't give them anything," said Jeff, in a whisper. "This plane is flying away from China to the U.S. There's nothing they can do to you."

I pondered that. It hadn't been a consideration, but on its face seemed likely to be true. I was lucky the flight was not headed in the opposite direction.

The young woman's polite smile was fading as she lost patience. She extended her hand toward me to receive the passport.

From the row behind us, the two gentlemen who'd been most offended by the event were stewing and their guttural curses were growing louder. Their protests were echoed by other passengers around us. The middle-aged woman across the aisle from me was shooting me laser darts of shame with her eyes and I had the distinct impression she wanted the flight attendant to be more assertive with me. I hadn't been this full of angst since I nearly burned down my elementary school, thirty years earlier.

"Sir," she said again, "you really must give me your passport, it's only right."

Phrasing it this way, as an ethical question, helped me decide. "Xiao-jie," I said.

Jeff elbowed me.

"Miss," I began again. He was right, my Chinese wasn't good enough to use it in this high-stakes discussion. "I'm not sure what is right in this case."

She looked puzzled. "You know what's right. You broke his violin." She pointed to the man behind me, who emphasized the point by jostling my seatback.

That, too, was clarifying. I was now being bullied into taking responsibility for the man's violin having been cracked. It had dropped out of the overhead bin I'd opened to retrieve my carry-on bag.

The 'fasten seatbelt' light had been off. I'd opened the bin cautiously, as I always do, and nothing had looked too concerning. I gently took my bag out of the bin. At that moment, we'd hit a big air pocket. I fell backward into the aisle. Some coats and jackets that had been placed lovingly around the violin case fell onto my legs followed by a dark object that landed with some force, hitting the floor and my left foot. It was the violin case.

The violin's owner jumped up. I did the same, and quickly closed the bin before anything else came flying out. He wore simple, unbranded clothing that I'd come to recognize as standard attire from the interior provinces of China. It was almost certainly his first trip outside the country. He popped the metal latches and opened the case.

A hairline crack ran just beside where the upper bout meets the neck. He studied it with bewilderment, his mouth open. Then he looked up at me.

"I'm so sorry," I said. "What can I do?"

I'm sure he didn't understand, but he shook his head, recognizing that my body language was communicating the right message. It was an accident.

Then his buddy started talking in angry protest. The other passengers around us echoed the tone. Then, and only then, did the violin's owner give me a grimace. That's when the flight attendant walked up.

"Strap in," said Jeff. "That was a big bump."

The flight crew hadn't said anything over the PA about turbulence. The seatbelt sign remained off. My distraction level was very high. I was focused on the cataclysm of the cracked musical instrument. Still, Jeff was right. I sat and buckled up.

The flight attendant leaned into the row behind me, listening to the tale of woe that I was experiencing myself all too forcefully, while the plane began bucking and jumping. The pilot now announced it was time to strap in. The flight attendant paid no heed and had turned to me to harangue me for my passport.

"I don't know what's right in this case," I repeated.

"Since you broke his violin," she said, "you must pay for it."

OK, I thought, that makes a little sense, but with my passport?

"Bullshit," muttered Jeff. "The airline has to pay."

He was, of course, absolutely right. The airline was responsible for damages incurred to passenger luggage while under the care of their aircrew. I recognized that was a subtle, and perhaps not at all Chinese, legal perspective. It might be right, but it wasn't going to help.

Still, the resolve to hang onto my passport had solidified into a fortress.

"Miss," I informed her, "I will pay for his violin."

Jeff gave a grunt of complete disgust, which I ignored.

"Very good," she said, "please, your passport."

"I will never give you my passport. Instead, I will give you my phone number. You can give it to him," I gestured behind me. "When we get to Los Angeles, he can get a quote on the repair or replacement of his violin, then call me. I'll pay it."

She looked uncertain, then explained to the violin owner. There were howls of protest from all around me. It felt like a rebellion was about to break out.

"Sir," she pleaded, "how can he trust you?"

"Because I've given my word," I said. "And by the way…" I then gave her a short lecture about how SHE should be handing over her phone number and the airline should be cutting the poor guy a check. I could see it flew over her head, so I returned to my point.

"My word is more valuable than a passport," I said. I wrote my name and number on a scrap of paper. She reluctantly gave it to the man. There were many additional howls of protest.

"Chess?" asked Jeff, now looking very content.

"We don't have a chess set," I pointed out. Jeff

fixed that with the remaining scrap of paper I'd used, cutting it into 32 tiny pieces with his fingernails, and meticulously coloring half of them black and writing a single tiny letter to indicate their prominence. This took about 20 minutes while the maelstrom continued to roil, but with slowly lessening force.

During this time the flight attendant did her best to calm the crowd. She finally caught on that the seatbelt light had come on, and worked diligently to divert the riled passengers' attention to the importance of strapping in and buckling up.

Jeff used his paperback book to scrawl straight lines and squares to represent the chessboard on a second piece of paper. We began to play makeshift chess.

An hour later, he'd won two of three games. The cabin was quiet, the lights dim. People drifted off to sleep.

A week after we landed in Los Angeles I got a call from a young woman who explained that Mr. Chao's violin repair cost $75. "I can send you the quote," she said.

"No need," I said. "Just tell me where to send the check." I like to think that Mr. Chao is still playing that violin. I hope he puts it under his seat on all future flights.

OULU, FINLAND – 1997

Bunk Mates

Hold the moose!

It didn't feel like we could go any further north in this blinding gray land, but my map said otherwise. Northern Finland in January can be a very foreboding place. We'd long since left behind the relative Eden of alternating flat, forested lands punctuated with the blue flatness of lakes, each seemingly with a single rustic cabin on its shore.

"Every family has a summer getaway cabin," explained Toivo. "They are all surrounded by forest and on the shore of a lake." There had to be a million lakes in this country of stern and formal people, whose warmth and charm were most definitely hiding far below a grim and stoic exterior. Once I learned how to tap that warmth, I quickly grew to admire the Finns.

With a population of four million, an average family size of four, and one cabin on the shore of every lake, the math worked well. With that lovely bit of Finland behind us, we were now in a land that grew more austere and alien with each passing kilometer, as we raced Toivo's diesel Volkswagen Rabbit up the thin, black asphalt strip, toward the globally recognized citadel of mobile phone technology – the Nokia design center in Oulu. The pine trees grew shorter and finally were dwarfed by the scrub of the tundra, which itself quickly disappeared.

Oulu. Like all Finnish words and names, if you say the word without smashing the hardest possible accent on the "O" then you aren't speaking correctly. The rest of the town's name was pronounced "Lou." Correctly enunciated, any non-Finn would assume you'd just been gut-punched precisely at your solar plexus. Industry legend had it that 10,000 brilliant design engineers were essentially exiled to Oulu so they could focus on creating the next generation of the world's greatest communications devices and infrastructure. Just 200 kilometers (130 miles) south of the Arctic Circle, there wasn't much happening in Oulu. The joke was that you designed hard because there wasn't anything else to do.

The short winter daylight evaporated as we finally approached the town. The amazing technology wrought by Nokia came to life with bright LEDs lighting up Toivo's dashboard – his mobile phone was ringing.

"Hello," he said, his tall, lanky frame still leaning forward to peer into the gloom; it wasn't always obvious when that little strip of asphalt might drift left or right. I was glad I wasn't was driving.

A female voice was rattling away over the speaker. "Keskusta!" Toivo suddenly shouted, although it might have been something totally different; my command of Finnish is functionally zero. Knowing "lingonberry vodka" in English was all I ever needed.

He was clearly upset as he shouted a stream of Finnish invective back at the phone. This went on for several minutes. When he slowed down, the female voice would interject a one-syllable sound with an extremely harsh accent on its only syllable. Finally, Toivo took a deep breath, and said, "Ok, thank you."

"All good?" I asked.

Toivo emitted some kind of deep primitive guttural noise that began in his abdomen and rolled slowly with a few gurgles up his esophagus and emerged mostly from his nostrils as something between a burp and a hiss.

"The hotel has only one room for us," he said. "I'm very sorry." It quickly followed that there weren't any other hotel rooms available anywhere in Oulu, which meant for hundreds of kilometers in any direction, of course.

"Oh, and the room has only one bed."

It was then the Oulu smell struck me. A putrid, tar smell. "We are close," he said. "I can smell the bay." Great.

"No problem, Toivo," I said. "We'll get some extra blankets and I'll sleep on the floor."

"No!" he shouted. "No! It's not acceptable for you, the guest, to be treated this way."

"It's fine by me." He would hear none of it.

We rolled into town, and at the hotel front desk there was yet another display of Finnish language being loudly and harshly exchanged between Toivo and the young uniformed desk clerk. It sounded like civil war to me, but in fact both were smiling and nodding politely throughout.

"Good news, Tim. The restaurant is still open, if we go now we can eat."

Now that was good news. It was a typical Finnish dinner buffet, heavy on the herring but replete with salmon, blini, and some rather tasty reindeer stew. I was happy as a clam.

Until we went to our room.

The single bed filled it, almost wall-to-wall with hardly space to scoot around to go into a tiny bathroom, which itself was so small that it combined toilet vanity and shower with a single plastic door to shield the bedroom from whatever activity went on there. Essentially, there was no floor space. We were both going to be sleeping in one bed.

Toivo's face was ashen. "We can sleep reverse," he suggested. The thought of his huge feet in my face all night was not computing.

"Grab that side," I said. I took the other. We both gave a mighty pull, and by god that little bed flew apart into two very tiny beds, with the sound of some kind of spinning metal winding down on the hardwood floor – we'd busted the bolts securing the frame. Separated by about four inches, it was a vast gulf of isolation to us both. We quickly got the front desk to give us separate sheets and blankets.

The young woman who delivered them made some aggressive noises at Toivo, then dumped her load and quickly left.

"Problem?"

"She said we broke their bed and will be charged," said Toivo.

"Put it on my tab." We slept so close that if either of us had sneezed the other would have been wiping snot off his face, but it was a highly acceptable solution. Of course, we weren't charged extra the next morning when we checked out and went to the Nokia design center.

The Nokia team was happy to see us. I suppose they were happy to see anyone who came to visit them in this wintry desolation. We had a great session, secured our design win, and politely begged off lunch. "We have a long journey ahead," Toivo pointed out.

The lead engineer walked us back to the parking lot. "I'll get you a taxi to the airport."

"No need," said Toivo. "We drove."

The engineer stared, speechless. "You drove a car from Helsinki to Oulu in winter?"

Toivo smiled and nodded.

"You guys are very dedicated, but that's crazy. Be careful on the drive home."

"We will," assured Toivo.

"Be careful of moose," the engineer said, waving good-bye.

"There's that word again," I said. "Moose."

Toivo sighed deeply. On a previous trip with Toivo and my boss, Toivo had been driving down a stark black highway. When my boss had conversationally mentioned the word "moose" Toivo had slammed on the brakes and brought the car to a slippery halt. "Where? Where's the moose?" When he learned there was no moose, he'd then lectured us on how more Finns are killed by impacts with moose than any other accidental cause. He'd finished: "Never say 'moose' unless you see a moose."

"Tim, I told you once. Please never say that word again. Unless you see one!"

FINLAND – 1998

Scandinavian Switchback

The Finnish army is the only army to defeat Stalin's in war.

Just for cultural context, the Russian Red Army invaded Finland in the winter of 1939. I mean, why not? Hitler had already taken half of Poland and invited Stalin to lap up the rest of it in a few short weeks that September. It had gone so swimmingly for the Russian Man of Steel, that he issued an ultimatum, which the Finns duly rejected.

What was a murderous egomaniacal dictator to do? Invade, of course. He sent a million under-armed, under-provisioned, and poorly led Russian soldiers into the forests and lakes of Finland, where they were picked off by well-hidden snipers or surrendered in droves to an adept force of Finns perhaps 10% its size, most whom nimbly arrived to the fight on cross-country skis.

The combination of being blocked by the Finnish army and waking to the probability that he was to be Hitler's next victim, compelled Stalin to 'permit' the nation of Finland to survive and negotiate a mutually unhappy, yet sovereign, peace. When the war went in Germany's favor, the Finns retook ceded lands, and when the mighty Red Army juggernaut began to polish off a broken German Wehrmacht, the memory of Finnish resolve again kept the Finns free of Soviet domination. World War II ended with Finland still sovereign.

This is only one reason I believe the Finns are among the toughest people anywhere.

I've long considered Finland my third home, not that I've spent much time there; but it made a dent on me. I've made maybe eight or nine trips, each lasting about ten days. Close proximity to many Finnish folks gave me an appreciation of the land and its people, all 4 million of them.

It didn't happen overnight. In fact, it definitely took some getting used to. First, there's the famous Finnish lack of emotion. At first impression, it seemed a land of Vulcans, each tidily unaware of the human imperative to express joy, pain, or sorrow. Critically for me, the Finns seemed to be left cold by my nonchalant and ever-present attempts at humor.

I may not always be cracking jokes and quipping, but I'm always – especially when I'm on a sales call – thinking about my next skewed observation designed to at least elicit an uncomfortable laugh. That's how I try to develop a bond that, hopefully, builds the relationship. For me, it's like drawing a saw rapidly backward on a tree branch; that first little break in the bark is pretty safe, and it's also pretty certain. With time, that branch is sure to drop.

With the Finns, on that long first trip, I couldn't get a read. My saw blade seemed dreadfully dull. In fact, Finnish people have a great sense of humor, hidden deep behind a hardened reserved exterior shell. I found that I had to warm that shell considerably. Sometimes it would take hours before they would open up and enjoy themselves, and begin speaking freely, or even laugh. Of course, drinking their very tasty lingonberry vodka accelerates the warming process.

It was after dinner one night with a group of eight Nokia engineers in the far north of Finland that I cracked the code, so much so that they suggested sauna. Sauna is not extraordinary. Most homes in Finland have a sauna and it's family tradition to take off one's clothes, get in the sauna, and continue the evening's banter. Mom, dad, kids. It's the one time that modesty is a non-factor and I quickly found to my surprise that the situation was no different among Finnish business folk.

We entered the establishment, hung up our coats, entered the locker room, disposed our remaining garments, right down to the well, right down to the birthday suit, and scooted into the sauna itself, which was a fabulous construct made from traditional materials: rock, straw and snow. In the center of the igloo-shaped room was the fire – a huge pile of glowing stones and embers generating significant heat. Around it were buckets of water with long silver ladles.

We made ourselves comfortable sitting around the fire on logs that were warm to the touch, and warm on, shall we say, our naked exposed seats. Occasionally one of the Nokia guys would ladle up water and jets of steam would come hissing out of the fire. The room was toasty and moist. The company was excellent. We were eight men all in the same basic work, all having had a little too much lingonberry vodka, chatting about whatever struck our fancy.

Several of the Nokia guys picked up branches, or switches, and casually swatted those next to them. It actually felt really good, and my back was flushed with the warmth of additional circulation. Before long I was handed a switch and returned the favor to those beside me.

Then one of them, we'll call him Anti, because, in fact, that was his name, announced that it was a good time to have some more vodka. He looked around then reached behind him and found a long rope attached to which was a bell.

Anti gave it a jangle and within a few minutes, the entrance way to the sauna opened and in walked a young woman. She had to be the most beautiful Scandinavian woman I had ever set eyes upon. She had long flowing red hair, a tightly fitted apron, red lipstick, and perfectly applied black mascara making her blue eyes azure sink-holes. She was a classic Scandinavian goddess.

The room fell silent. I personally felt more than a little embarrassment, but I don't think I was alone. She asked Anti. "What would you like to drink?" in some strange language, that I took to be Finnish. I've never had a feel for it. Have I mentioned that if you want to speak Finnish, you need to put a hard accent on the first syllable of EV-ry SING-le WOR-d? You do. Anti answered for us, "Lingonberry vodka." She left the room and returned a few minutes later, pushing a small cart. She said nothing.

We said nothing either, as she poured the vodka for each of us into long crystal stem glasses. Once she was done, she gave us a little nod. It seemed to signal to the group some kind of demarcation. It was a sign that we could now exhale, enjoy our vodka, and relax again. She pushed the cart out of the room and closed the door. It was at this point that Anti said, "Well gentlemen. There is every reason to celebrate."

We raised our glasses. Eight, naked, defenseless geeky men were once again marginally comfortable in their own company. It's not a bad way to pass a frozen night near the Arctic Circle.

CALIFORNIA GOLD COUNTRY – 1998

Fool's Gold

Pans, picks and shovels. Just add water.

Thump!

"Dag nammit!" I cursed loudly. A squirrel had just darted out of the grass on the left side of the highway. I'd had less than a second to react, and had tried to steer such that the poor creature might pass safely between our left and right sets of wheels. The jolt told me that he hadn't made it.

"What happened?" my wife, Shelly, asked from the backseat.

I did not hesitate. "Nothing, dear. Just hit a little bump in the road." I looked over to shotgun where Chris was impassively nodding his head in agreement.

"Gotta watch out for those bumps," he said, preserving my cover story.

We drove at an exhilarating pace up the long, straight highway that led toward California's Gold Country. Tonight, we'd domicile at a bed and breakfast nestled in the very same hills where Marshall and Sutter had discovered the first gleaming glints in the American River. The river itself is a fine rafting venue that pours out of the tall, granite Sierra Nevada mountains. That was in 1848, and while the men tried to keep the discovery secret, by 1849 the world was beating a path to California, seeking their fortune.

The California Gold Rush is the stuff of legend. Those who have studied this phenomenon have concluded that while some fortunes were indeed made, most of them were in selling picks and shovels, food and staples to the miners. What little gold they panned from the river often was lost at the gambling tables and makeshift brothels that chased the miners and their meager earnings with a vengeance. Swindlers, often disguised as bankers, would weigh, measure, and assay the purity of the gold – factoring the greed or desperation in the eye of the seller – and hand over far less than market value in cash. Many, ill-prepared for the journey, died en route.

Those who did survive, whether they made their fortunes or lost them, realized they had come to the right place. California, if I may say so as a third generation native, is one fabulous place to live. Travelling to distant lands is a passion of mine, but one thing that makes these journeys even more enjoyable is the expectation of returning to the rolling hills, redwood forests, rugged coastlines and craggy mountains of my origins. The Dead Kennedys said it well: California uber alles! Even after the onslaught of decades of relative drought that caused the hills to trade much of their green for brown, California was beautiful.

As we approached gold country, I was excited by the prospect of trying my hand at panning up at least a few glints of the yellow stuff. I'd done this as a kid in the Boy Scouts. A would-be 49er wades into the rushing waters, digs a metal pan into the deep silt, and sifts out the sand to try to isolate the heavy gold, which will sink to the bottom of the pan.

While I never discovered a gold nugget, the motivation to keep trying was bright and glinting in the mountain sunlight – hundreds and thousands of golden flecks, sparkling like glitter, were the tell-tale confirmation that gold was present. Even the knowledge that some of these were pyrite – fool's gold, which is equally shiny but of no value – did not diminish my ardor for the hunt. Some of these flecks were gold, and where flecks of gold existed, nuggets are present too. A few of the other scouts did find large chunks of pyrite (proven not be gold with a simple weight and density test). That was never the point: the thrill was in the chase.

On this trip, I'd been adamant that we make a quick stop, at least, to do some panning. I'd read about a spot that had been the center of a major gold mining camp back in the 1850s. It was directly on the path to our lodging. Some of our coterie, Chris most vocal among them, had loudly proclaimed that it was all a fool's errand, a waste of valuable time that we could instead use tasting at many of the prolific gold country wineries. I was not to be dissuaded, however. Plus I was driving.

"Looks like we're approaching your gold camp," said Chris, studying our detailed map of the region. "You sure about this, Jenkins? A lot of the wineries start closing at 4:00pm, so it's a trade-off."

"A worthy one, I can assure you," I informed him. "I'm the only one in this vehicle who has enjoyed the thrill that the 49ers felt. Now, all of you, get to share that same excitement."

From the back seat, I heard a groan of resignation. "Fool's errand," Chris repeated. "But OK then. At least we can find a picnic spot. You'll want this turn-off coming up." We approached a little road forking off the main one, with a sign that proclaimed 'Campo Seco.'

"That's it," I said. "It's name in the gold rush day was Camp Collins, named for the first miner who struck his fortune here."

"Why the name change?" asked Chris.

"Reverting back to the original Spanish?" I ventured. "Not sure."

The road to Campo Seco was rugged. The SUV jolted and bounced as we passed ancient gnarled oaks and dry scrub grass. We entered the camp. We knew we'd arrived due to the decaying remnants of several wooden buildings – the miners had stayed for years, such was their haul – and had converted from tents to cabins. The biggest remaining structure still had a sign on it: "Ge—l Store". Some of the letters had fallen away after 140 years under the punishing central California sun.

"OK, Jenkins," said Chris. "Where do we pan?"

He had a great question. We'd come downhill quite some way, and I fully expected the camp would be located here, at the lowest point, which would also include the rapidly flowing stream, where the miners had dug their pans.

"Not sure," I said.

"What's this place again?" asked someone in the back seat. I looked in the rearview mirror and saw it was Hailey, Chris's wife.

"Camp Collins," I told her. "More recently, Campo Seco."

"Campo Seco?" she repeated. "Doesn't that mean "dry camp" in Spanish?"

I don't know much Spanish. I know a few basics. I should know more. Huevos Rancheros. Taqueria. Cerveza, por favor. I'm equipped only with the important bare minimum.

So while not conversant in Spanish, I do have very clear vision. "Hmm. This does look like the driest place we've seen. Let's stop up there, at that plaque."

I parked the vehicle and we stretched our legs. Chris marched directly to the plaque, and read it aloud. "Here marks the former spot of Camp Collins, a long defunct gold camp. Originally named Campo Seco by the earliest Spanish explorers, this site is known for its many long decades of dry spells. The water the '49ers encountered was a part of an uncharacteristic wet spell, the likes of which haven't been seen since."

"Hmm," I said, somewhat at a loss. "Dang."

Chris turned on his heel and marched back toward the vehicle. "As I said. A fool's errand. Let's eat lunch at that picnic bench." He swatted away a huge, black fly that was buzzing his nose. It did look like a nice spot, under a large, gnarled oak tree.

As we unpacked our plowman's lunch of cheese, salami, and baguettes, more of those big flies buzzed us. "Jesus," someone said, "I almost ate a fly." The buggers were swarming, so we ate quickly.

"Let's leave this place to the Lord of the Flies," Chris quipped, and tossed a piece of salami, hoping to distract some of the flying bastards. "We might still catch an open winery."

I put my useless tail between my legs and happily drove us to the winery. It was still open, and we were the last party admitted for tasting that day. After the fourth wine, the owner -- our pourer -- asked what we were doing in gold country.

"Looking for gold," said Chris. "Of course."

The owner laughed. "Ha! Good luck with that. We've got fool's gold, but not much real gold anymore."

Chris didn't needle me further. I ventured, "Well, this Chardonnay has a buttery flavor and a golden hue. I think this is the gold we were really seeking."

"Indeed," said Chris. "Here's to the '49ers."

IN FLIGHT OVER THE NORTH ATLANTIC – 2000

The Accidental Upgrade

Some good deeds do go unpunished.

After all those trips to Scandinavia and northern Europe, I finally had some status on KLM, the flagship carrier of the Netherlands. If you want to enjoy an extreme level of flight attendant militancy, KLM is definitely the airline for you. Like the Dutch themselves, they are feisty and not the least bit shy. Overall, I have to say it's a good way to fly.

This turned out to be, and I was already pretty sure it would be, the last of my European junkets for this company. After three years and perhaps 20 Atlantic crossings, I'd identified a new shiny object on my career path. When this flight touched down in Los Angeles, I would not go home. Rather, I would be jumping on another plane for San Francisco, then driving to the Sonoma County town of Santa Rosa for a job interview. There was something happening there. They called it "Telecom Valley."

That meant I really needed sleep, and was glad of my aisle row emergency exit seat with extra room. Shortly after the first meal was served, I slumped in my seat and began dream-weaving.

It didn't last long. I awoke to a sharp pain in my right kneecap. Something hard had just landed on it. My eyes opened into the brown, vacant eyes of a man who lay across my lap, his legs splayed out into the aisle. I instinctively cupped his head in my right hand and steadied him with my left.

"Are you ok?" I asked. His gaze seemed sightless, his breathing labored. I looked over to my neighbor in the middle seat, who was sound asleep. The lady next to him was reading a magazine and minding her own business. I looked up. I couldn't reach the call button without dumping the poor guy.

"Pardon me," I asked her. She flipped a page. "Pardon! Excusez-moi!"

She looked over. "Oh!" She jumped up and pushed the call button.

The blue uniformed flight attendant strolled up and asked, "What are you doing?"

I let that go. "It seems this man has fainted. He fell into my seat. He needs a doctor."

She leaned in close to study him. "OK, wait."

Two more flight attendants arrived. Another's voice rang out on the PA system: "Hello, if you are a doctor, please come now to row 45. Thank you."

No doctors arrived, but a very strange man with disheveled hair and crooked necktie did. "You," he grunted at me. "You---"

"Yes? Is this your friend?"

He struggled to say something, but a flight attendant brushed him aside. "We need to give him aspirin," she said. "We need to find aspirin." It was a good idea in case he'd had a heart attack. I have no idea why the airline didn't have any for such an occasion.

"Hand me the black backpack right above me," I said. She did so. I fumbled to get my keychain. It had a tiny container with two of almost every kind of medicine one might need. I unscrewed it, and still keeping the man's head cradled in my elbow, managed to spill out an aspirin. I handed it to the flight attendant.

She eye-balled it critically. "How do I know this is aspirin?" she asked, obviously skeptical. I didn't mean to be sarcastic with her, but....

"If you read what's on the pill," I said, "it says 'aspirin'."

Her blue eyes flashed, but she put her penlight on the pill, then nodded in satisfaction.

"Get up," she commanded. I was only too happy to comply. I helped her put the unconscious man in my seat. She and another attendant then inserted the aspirin in the poor man's mouth and a third pushed a cup of water forward. I wasn't so sure about this.

Water spilled down his shirt, but he did seem to be swallowing. That might have worked! He suddenly emitted an enormous cough, spraying everyone with fine droplets. Oh, well.

The disheveled man approached me again. "You!" He said.

"Yes?"

"You, you should go back to your seat!" he hissed. At this point, I concluded the man was drunk or on some kind medication.

"I'd like that, too," I pointed out. "But he's in my seat now." I gestured at the unconscious man. The disheveled man just shook his head. Another call for a doctor came over the PA.

A man walked up. "Who needs help?" I pointed again to the poor guy in my seat, whose head was now lolling back and forth, right and left.

The man who might actually be a doctor did a really smart thing. He kneeled down, took the man's hand and began to feel for pulse. The guy looked awful, but at least it seemed now he finally had competent help.

I felt a hand on my elbow. "This way, sir," said the blue-eyed attendant, with what can only be called a more pleasant tone. She nonetheless shuffled me forward down the aisle rather forcibly. I held up a finger. "Backpack?"

"I'll bring it to you promptly," she said. That was good enough for me.

Feeling like a ten year old who's stolen candy, I was pushed past the business class curtain to row 11.

"Sit here." I did so.

"Hi," said a young Asian woman. "I heard someone is sick on the plane," she said. I confirmed that for her, and gave her my summary.

"My gosh," she said, "the airline should give you an award."

Without giving it any further thought, I informed her: "I believe they already have, assuming you don't mind my sitting here?" She laughed. My backpack arrived. My new seatmate ordered champagne. I got no more sleep but we ate well, drank well, and had a great time exchanging stories of the road, life, and everything.

The poor guy who crashed into my knee? That doctor did something right. Upon landing in Los Angeles, the stricken man was escorted off the plane first, while all other passengers were asked to wait. He looked unsteady but staggered off the plane under his own power, with a little help. It was the same man who kept saying "You!" but now he was smiling, and even waved to me as he was ushered past.

The whole incident seemed a bit mysterious. I pondered it on my connecting flight to San Francisco and the drive north to Sonoma County. But by the next morning, I was busy meeting people in a telecommunications start-up company that became my focus for the next five years.

A career segue earmarked by an accidental upgrade caused by an enigma. I suppose.

GANDHI MODE

SOUTHERN CHINA – 2003

The $45 Million Dollar Hoax

Trust, but verify. Mostly verify.

Our company's next big demo was in Hong Kong, and it felt like time for me to get out of the office. We'd begun talks with a gigantic partner, customer, and potential suitor, who was famous the world over for their mobile communications gear. It had its sights set on acquiring us to plug a hole in their portfolio. Suddenly, in the midst of the worst telecommunications meltdown in history, things were looking up for us.

The frightening SARS epidemic in China had only just faded, and air tickets to Asia were consequently cheap. It was a very good time to travel.

The largest telecom carrier in Hong Kong was hosting our gear. I went with one of my technical guys, a counterpart in the partner company, and one of his technical guys. We four ate well, drank well, and did our job. The two technical guys actually had to work. We business guys did our usual meet, greet, and hob-nob.

Having flown halfway around the world to get here, I thought that once the demo was a success, the least I could do was to check in with our first and only China customer: NewTel. They were a short train ride away in nearby Guangzhou.

The purchase order from NewTel had come in a few months back, on the very last day of the fiscal year, New Year's Eve, shortly before midnight in California, the last possible minute to qualify as revenue for the year. For all of $38,000, it wasn't much – a partial system that didn't have the minimal redundancy required in the telecom world.

The last minute timing was no coincidence. Just over a year prior to receipt of this order, Dirk -- our VP of Sales -- had hired a salesman to cover Asia, particularly China. His name was Newton, and he lived in eastern Canada – almost as far from China as one can get. I bumped into Dirk and Newton on Newton's first day. Dirk, who famously ran his own show, tried to wave me off on their way to some other meeting. But I wanted to meet the new guy – whose arrival had been a well-kept secret.

I introduced myself and shook hands with Newton. "Newton's going to be racking up sales in China within a month," said Dirk, by way of bragging what a savvy recruiter he was.

"That's great," I said. And then in Chinese: "Welcome aboard!" To which Newton looked very uncomfortable. He said nothing. Odd.

Newton's first week ended with the company's annual sales meeting and celebration at a fabulous Italian restaurant. Even with the telecom bubble popping, we had some victories to celebrate, and our top sales guy, Rand, was given a special award. He was praised by three executives in short, successive speeches followed by a toast. Rand doesn't smile much, but he looked happy.

"I would like to say," said Newton, standing up with his glass and a toast of his own. "That these numbers by Rand, while good, will be nothing compared to what we'll see from China in the coming year." His face was all grins. This was the guy who had just arrived a few days prior.

I was watching Rand. He didn't look so happy now. Nobody did.

"In fact," said Newton, "I'll be delivering a minimum $45 million from China, and then you'll all be toasting *me* at this event next year." He raised his glass. Only a few folks joined him. It was an uncouth boast – the kind people don't easily forget.

Which is why, one year later, as midnight closed in and the solitary NewTel purchase order for a lousy $38,000 had slithered in at the final bell, the sum total of Newton's boast was coming home to roost. He'd made perhaps a dozen trips to Asia that first year, all of them on business class tickets. His expense reports were fat envelopes full of smeared Chinese script. He listed $350 a night hotels, but no Hyatt or Hilton gold embossed envelopes accompanied these claims. The accounts payable administrator, Lynn, was so furious with his obvious pilfering of the corporate largesse, that she slammed a packet of receipts one day on my desk.

"You read Chinese!" she said. "Tell me what these are."

My Chinese isn't that good, but I let my wife review them that night. "These are all from one of those cheap receipt books they sell at 7-11," she informed me. "Anyone can fill them out for anything they want. I've never seen a $400 hotel bill on one of *these* before." She held it up as if it were rare Greek parchment. When I reported this back to Lynn, it was not a happy moment.

"This is ridiculous," she said. "I'm going to talk to Dirk about this." She did, but it came to naught.

Now, fifteen months after Newton's hire, I stepped off the train station platform and met his one and only customer, Frank. He was a congenial fellow who made sunny small talk on the ride to the NewTel office. On the sixth floor of his building, we entered an office labeled "WesTech Networks."

"Did you guys change names?" I asked.

Frank presented his business card, two-handed. It was a WesTech card. "No, we've always been WesTech. Very famous in Guangdong province." He smiled. More of his team filed in and shook hands. All had WesTech cards.

Later, I worked into the conversation: "Just curious, why the purchase order we got from you guys in December says NewTel?"

"Purchase order?" asked Frank. "We promised Newton we'd evaluate your gear. We'll send it back good as new, but to be honest we're so busy it's still sitting in the boxes. What's NewTel?" No NewTel. No purchase order. No $45 million in year one.

"By the way," said Frank. "We were surprised to meet Newton. He's a very nice guy, but he doesn't speak a word of Chinese."

A complete hoax. This was bad enough. It got worse.

HANGZHOU, CHINA – 2003

The Smoke-Filled Room

Where deals are supposed to be made.

Shortly after my return from Hong Kong and Guangzhou, I handed Lynn my expense report. "Oh, by the way," I said, "here's *my* hotel bill." It was neatly typed in English and folded meticulously on thick hotel stationery stock. It was in a gold envelope. "You'll note it's less than a hundred U.S."

"Shove it!" We were both laughing. By now, she'd given up on Newton. She'd complained to Dirk and heard the "hey, pressures of the road, gotta take care of the customer" arm-waving speech too many times to care anymore.

The telecom bubble meltdown had reached new depths. After nearly two years of downward spiral, so many companies were dead that the few survivors actually began to show prospects. Our big suitor for the Hong Kong demo had now been joined by two more.

One was an ultra-aggressive cultural hybrid. The founder and CEO was born in Taiwan, raised in Japan, and totally American. He had created a juggernaut with successful products from mobile phone handsets to optical routers and access gear. He was only missing one thing in his portfolio, and we had built the best one of those out there.

It was deal time. First, we private-labeled our product for them, as we had with our big U.S. partners. UVTechcom had some high-powered engineers developing something like our gear, but it was slow, difficult, and they simply didn't have the depth of talent we commanded.

What they did have, in boatloads, was cash and a stock that was soaring while the likes of Nortel, Marconi, and Lucent were diving into uncharted depths. They made it very clear they were ready, willing and able to burn a little bit of that cash buying our company.

It turned out that a little bit was roughly $700 million. All the founders and most of the early employees would walk away with stacks of cash, in addition to most of them receiving a UVTechcom badge and all the benefits that a large, publicly traded company had to offer. I'd be able to build my long dreamt-of backyard swimming pool.

Those of us who had been looking closely at the deal trend lines saw this as perhaps the last chance for a lucrative "liquidity event" in which our crazy levels of effort and sweat would be rewarded. A few years back, Competitor A had sold for an insane $7 billion; a year later, company B sold for $3.2 billion; competitor C had almost closed a $1 billion deal two months ago, but missed it, and was now in receivership. Thirty or more similar companies were now dead. Valuations were tanking. This was our last best shot.

With an air of high-tension and high-promise, our CTO (Han) and VP of Operations (Ken) flew to Hangzhou, China, where UVTechcom had the bulk of its R&D, all of its manufacturing, and many of its top executives – all under one roof. The largest enclosed space in Asia, it couldn't have more closely resembled the Blofeld secret headquarters of 007 fame if it had been designed by Ian Fleming himself.

Upon arrival, they received the total VIP treatment. There were meetings, sure, but there was food, drink, and merriment in floods. Both of our executives had their first real exposure to KTV – Karaoke' – which, if you haven't tried, I recommend you add to your bucket list.

The third night was all business. The UVTechcom execs, all Chinese or Japanese nationals, were drinking expensive scotch and smoking. Our guys kept their heads on and focused. They stuck to their checklist. They had terms and conditions of merger, valuation, parachute contingencies, and the long view of product strategy and integration on their minds.

Johnny was the UVTechcom lead. He pounded the table a lot. He pounded it if he didn't like what was said. He pounded it a lot harder if he DID like it. The deal was sewing up as midnight approached; afternoon in California. Johnny had a single sheet of terms, a price tag and all the basics laid out. He scrawled his signature and slid it across to Ken.

Ken didn't need to look down at the paper. He knew what it contained: 100% of the checklist items they had been asked to get. The deal was closing. He looked up at Johnny who was now lighting the largest cigar Ken had ever seen.

Ken flipped open his phone. "Hey, Wes, how's it going?"

In California, our CEO had been anxiously awaiting this call. "Going fine, sounds like the Eagle has landed."

"Yes," said Ken. "We've got the valuation and the terms. Ok to sign?"

"I can't imagine why not, let me get Clare, Dirk, and Clint in here. I'll put you on speaker."

All the execs jammed into Wes's office. "Ok, guys," said Wes into the speakerphone, "tell us one more time what you got."

Ken did so.

"Shit, Wes," said Clint. "They did it."

Clare nodded approvingly. It added up.

Dirk, our VP sales, stood in the doorway and asked. "Hey, guys, how you feeling right now?"

Back in Hangzhou, Ken and Han looked at each other. Johnny exhaled an enormous stream of purple cigar smoke.

"Hey, Dirk, we're feeling really good. How about you?"

"Oh, hey, yeah, I'm great. Let me just give Newton a quick call."

Ken's face showed Johnny that he was ready for a little more scotch. Johnny leaned across the table and poured the 25 year old Yamazaki. It was quiet. Too quiet for Johnny.

"Hey Ken," he said, raising his glass. "What's the rule about scotch?"

"Rule?" asked Ken, keeping the phone close to his ear. "What's the rule?"

Johnny laughed. "Your scotch should always....and I mean always..."

Meantime, back in California, Dirk was talking to his China salesman, Newton. Newton, of the idle $45 million boast that had come to naught. Newton, who was spending $20,000 per junket to China, but who hadn't sold one thing. Whose only purchase order had proven to be fraudulent. Who had boasted idly to the rest of the sales team in his first week of employment, with nothing to show more than a year later. And who was now suspected, by our accountant, of having a second and possibly third wife, house, and set of children in various cities in China. The China salesman who lived in eastern Canada and couldn't speak a word of Chinese.

"Oh, hey, wait a minute, Dirk," said Newton. "We're going to make so much money in China. We don't need these guys." The conversation went downhill from there. For some reason, Dirk doubled down on his mistake of hiring Newton, and allowed himself to be talked out of the deal.

In small companies, power structures are mysterious. In ours, it came down to just two guys: Dirk and Wes. Almost nothing could happen unless both were in agreement.

Back in Hangzhou, Johnny delivered the punch line regarding 25 year old scotch.

"Your scotch," he said, then paused to puff his cigar, and for effect. "Your scotch should *always* be older than your women!" Johnny pounded the table. Everyone laughed. Until they heard a throat clearing over the speaker to California.

"Oh, hey, Ken," said Wes. "The guys are talking this over. We're thinking you guys come home and we'll continue the conversation back here in HQ."

The single page sat in front of Ken. He had a

glass of expensive scotch in one hand, and a Caran d'Ache ballpoint pen – worth more than his house, Johnny had told him – in the other. It was a moment of ultimate surrealism. It took him time to put the pen down.

"OK, sure thing, Wes," he said.

The phones were hung up. The Hangzhou room was filled with smoke. Across the table, Ken faced Johnny, who was blowing smoke rings.

"Ok, guys," said Johnny. "Let's go to KTV." He didn't pound the table this time. It was the right thing to say. It was, in fact, the only thing to do.

The deal didn't close. It got away clean and never came back. UVTechcom eventually finished building their competitive product and made a modest success of it. Our company limped into an increasingly desolate future. The work and hours became more brutal, and the prospects for a payout faded rapidly away. Before long, the board of directors moved in, hired a hatchet man who disposed of every executive and director in the company, and started the whole thing over. Lots of employees lost their jobs.

My backyard swimming pool? Missing in action, you might say.

SHANGHAI – 2006

Talk to ME if you want to talk to HIM

Fun with stereotypes.

"Shanghai, baby!" said my co-worker, Rich, as our plane banked over the metropolis. He and I had been asked to attend the annual global sales conference in Hangzhou, China. We were the sales numbers and contracts guys; Rich covered the Americas, and I covered Asia-Pacific and India. It was a big global company, with headquarters in California, but with a huge factory and design center in Hangzhou, China.

Although ethnic Chinese from Burma, Rich is an all-American guy. He's a California kid through and through. As this would be his first trip to China, we planned a couple days in Shanghai, China's showcase city to the world, and our logical entry point with Hangzhou just a 70 minute express train away.

What I remembered most about my previous trips to Shanghai was the terrific pace of construction. Everything was new and shiny. One hundred-story skyscrapers were like cheap row houses in any U.S. town – seemingly countless, and many with novel architectural styles. The cumulative effect puts New York City and Chicago to shame, or, at least, makes those cities feel quaint in an old world way. Shanghai is nothing like that except, perhaps, for the Bund.

Even the Bund, with its European architecture of the early 20th century, has had modernity sprout in and around it. This was where the dominating European powers of France, Germany, and England, together with the U.S., had set up their shops along the gentle meander of the Huangpu river, the very heart and center of Shanghai.

This was the area Rich and I explored our first afternoon in Shanghai. Before long, we developed an appetite, and decided to troll the famous Nanjing East Road. Most notorious for its shopping, it was loaded with eateries from around the world.

It was a wide pedestrian-only causeway, dense with people. Most of them were Asian but there was a significant number of non-Asian faces as well. In any case, the little digital cameras in almost everyone's hands revealed that almost everyone here was a tourist.

The sun had set and the summer evening delivered perfect strolling weather. It was slow going, and not just due to the crowds of tourists. There were also innumerable free-lance hawkers.

"You want Rolex?" one of them said to me, opening his jacket to reveal many dozens of shiny watches.

"No thanks," I said. He persisted, walking sideways to keep up with me.

"Highest quality," he said. "Only 10,000 yuan."

I've never owned a Rolex. The main reason I haven't is that they cost $25,000 or more. This guy was offering me a "Rolex" for about a $1,000. In Thailand I'd purchased a few of these obvious fakes for about $6. There, we 'farang' referred to these as "Rollexes" -- pronouncing ROL as in "rollicking".

"Not interested," I affirmed.

"How much you pay?"

"Bu yau!" I informed him in Chinese, which translates in this instance as "don't want."

The peddler stopped in his tracks, a surprised look on his face.

"Dude!" said Rich. "Did you just tell him to f-off?" He was laughing. Before I could answer him, Rich was assaulted from the opposite quarter by another salesman.

It was another "Rollex" vendor. His jacket lining had an even more impressive number of shiny fake precision timepieces. He asked Rich in Chinese: "How much you want to pay?"

Rich gave him the universal gesture – open hands, shrugged shoulders. "Ha? Hey, buddy, I don't speak your language."

The salesman was not willing to accept such an answer. "OK," he said in Chinese, "you pay 500 yuan?"

I guess that rubbed me way, way wrong. As an obvious foreigner, the opening bid I got was 20 times more than Rich.

"Listen," I said to the hawker in the language he was using with my buddy. "He's not interested."

"Wahhh!" the salesman said. "Your Chinese is so good!" He said it in English.

"That's right," I said in Chinese. "And if you want to talk to HIM, you need to talk to ME."

At this, the Rollex salesman backed a step away

from Rich. He looked Rich over, up and down, from Adidas to crew-cut. "Oh," he said. "Oh, very good. VIP!" He smiled and gestured the way forward.

Rich and I took a few steps before stopping and doubling over in laughter. "Hey, man," he said, "I'm not sure what you told that guy, but keep it up." In seconds the next victim was at hand. He was just as shocked as the first two guys.

Sometimes, even a blind squirrel bumbles into an acorn. My rudimentary Chinese had finally paid off handsomely. After a great repast of Korean barbeque, we even caved in and bought a few "Rollicking Rollexes" for about $1/250^{th}$ of that first offer -- $5.00 each. Those are negotiation results that any "good-cop, bad-cop" team might envy.

Our Man In Manilla

Every company needs a guy like this in Manilla, or any city for that matter.

For some salespeople, sweat is 90% of the deal. For others, charm and talent is 90%. A rare few just put 180% into every deal.

Our man in Manilla, Genghis Jang, greeted me as I exited customs. We'd never met, but he knew how to connect. As I emerged into the humidity of the airport arrivals zone, with hundreds of people holding up signs with hotels, transport companies, and people's names in many different languages, I spotted Genghis right away.

He was holding a tiny chalkboard, upon which he'd scrawled "Tim." My eyes found him even before I'd wheeled out of the departing passengers only zone. He'd already spotted me. I read my name on the chalkboard, looked up, and our eyes locked.

Genghis resembled Blackbeard the Pirate: a dark, trim beard, and deep brown eyes that seemed decades older than his body, which was visibly well-muscled through his sport coat. He wore a sports coat? This was Manilla. Nobody wears a coat.

He gave a firm handshake. "Good flight?" he asked in a low baritone.

"Yeah," I told him, "aren't they all?"

Genghis gave me a light tap of affirmation on the shoulder and did not ask my permission to take the roller bag. He tossed it over his shoulder like it was a towel and pointed the way. "We've got a car." We scattered dozens of waiting hawkers and confused deplaners getting to the curb. Emerging out of the exit doors, my glasses were instantly fogged by the Philippine humidity. Genghis tossed my bag into the trunk. I felt the first beads of perspiration as we got into the backseat.

Genghis gave some quiet instruction to the driver. The air conditioner roared and cold air swept over me. The car pulled away from the curb.

"It's a short ride to the hotel," he said, "not much traffic right now."

"Alright, Genghis," I said. "I have to ask: how do you do it?"

He raised an eyebrow.

"Come on," I said. "Nobody else is wearing a coat in this town."

He gave a gentle chortle. "I would hope not, but I'm a salesman, after all."

He was a legendary one, at that. We'd talked a bit on the phone in the preceding weeks, leading up to this visit, during which we planned to close on a $70 million contract with the leading telecom provider in the Philippines. We'd discovered a common interest in military history. He was half Turk, and his grandfather had survived the British onslaught at Gallipoli in the First World War. His mother was from Taiwan. There was hardly a major language he couldn't speak. Already I could see that one thing for sure could be counted on: Genghis knew how to keep his cool. That proved to be very important.

My boss had given me a little insight: "You and Genghis will get the deal, no worries there. Just do what he says, don't be surprised by anything he does."

"No need to be unduly alarmed," Genghis said as we approached the hotel driveway. "We're having a little Abu Sayyaf problem."

I'd read about the terrorist group that was highly active in the Philippine southern island of Mindanao. I hadn't realized the threat alert level was so high here in Luzon.

Sure enough, uniformed guards stopped our car as we entered the hotel driveway. They wanted to see us, our passports, our backpacks, and the contents of our trunk. One of them knelt down and extended a long pole underneath our car, and swept it back and forth. It was a camera boom, and after close inspection of the vehicle's undercarriage, they concluded we were not concealing any explosive devices. We were waved onto the hotel reception drive.

Genghis chatted with me until I was safely checked in at the hotel front desk. "Look," he said, "we can sit and have a drink, but you're tired and we both know what needs to happen tomorrow. You know I'm the good cop here. That makes you the bad cop."

"That's why I'm here," I agreed. "Just call me 'Doctor No.'"

"Wish it were that easy," he stated flatly. "This

customer is not used to being pushed around by anybody. Except Haiwei, of course."

"We're going to deliver the harsh medicine in a much more constructive manner than Haiwei would."

"Yes, of course," said Genghis. "Though I suspect before the day is out there'll be plenty of blood on the floor. Rest up, my friend."

I already loved Genghis. He'd set my expectations for the worst. He used 'my friend' instead of 'buddy.' Lots of great sales people call their counterparts 'buddy' but to me it always feels a little bit like I'm being sold. There's no question that Genghis was closing on me, too. In contrast, his 'my friend' felt real. Tomorrow, we'd be in the same trench when the whistle blew and in our heads we'd picture the commander shouting, "Over the top, boys!" We'd fix bayonets and dutifully run toward the melee.

At the customer's headquarters the next morning, Marco kept us waiting. This was completely expected. This was, after all, the Philippines, and he was, after all, the customer. This particular customer, was determined to push us into complete and total compliance with his contract, the terms and conditions of which would act as a tourniquet around the neck of our company. That wasn't going to happen. Now to the little matter of explaining that to him.

"Tim, thanks for coming out to meet with us," said Marco, who wore typical Philippine business wear: a white button-down shirt with tab collar and neatly circular bottom hem, untucked of course. It looked far more comfortable than my long-sleeve white cotton. "Your redlines are unacceptable, so I'd like to ask you to withdraw them."

"Thanks, Marco," I said. "We really appreciate your time in seeing us today. Regarding our redlines, I'd like to walk through the top five issues and give you our rationale and some alternative recommended approaches."

"It's not acceptable to ever change our standard contract," he said a bit harshly. "So there's no need. We can never accept any change."

"I see," I informed Marco. "I understand. Since your time is very valuable, we won't waste it quibbling over details in that case. I would like to point out, however, that we can't sign the contract as is; but we have mapped out a solution we feel will be very attractive to you."

"No," said Marco. "We don't accept changes."

"These are options, Marco," I clarified. "If I can have five minutes—"

Genghis interrupted. "Marco."

I stopped. We both looked to Genghis. He sat relaxed in his chair. "Nobody in this room," he continued, "wants to see that other company in here again. You don't, more than any of us. You remember what they did to you last time?"

Marco's face visibly transformed into a red-rimmed grimace. "Don't tell me about them," he said. "We don't deal with them anymore."

"But you did before, and they never sat down to explain anything. They just told you what you do," ventured Genghis, who was truly crawling onto the longest, weakest limb I'd ever seen in a sales meeting with a key customer.

"We won't do that," he added quietly. "We'll work with you. We'll make this deal work for you."

Marco's face was red as a beet, but the epaulets on his white shirt shifted slightly toward his neck line, the tension in his shoulders collapsing. He seemed to be resigning himself to...something.

"Give Tim five minutes," said Genghis.

Marco said nothing, but he barely nodded 'yes'. I seized the moment.

"We have some ideas," I began, "that your team and management will appreciate." That was mostly spin, because in my allotted five minutes I explained why we would never, ever sign-up to the harsh penalties and legal cages in his contract. Somehow, I was now the good cop, and Genghis, though pushing his customer hard, also remained the good cop.

Essentially, we were telling poor Marco he could deal with the devil that had previously abused him without mercy, or deal with us – the devil who at least would face him, talk to him, and try to show him another way of doing business.

No, he wasn't happy, but after ninety minutes, he was satisfied. He had pushed back and we had agreed to yield some small points here and there. "I'll review and get back to you tomorrow," Marco said, standing and shaking our hands.

We walked into the Manilla heat.

"Genghis," I protested happily, "I came out here to be the bad guy."

"You did fine," he replied. "But that's just a lot of crap," he said. "The salesman must always be responsible for enforcing his customer's good behavior."

We got the deal and the customer was saved from himself, thanks to our man in Manilla.

NEW DELHI, INDIA – 2005

Taj Mahalin' It

Enjoy the journey, even if you don't arrive.

With the Philippines contract sewn up, my next stop was India, to iron out some wrinkles we were encountering from a huge deal we'd secured on my first visit there a few months back. An opportunity presented itself: fly back to California the way I'd come, or continue westward and do my first circumnavigation of the globe. I'm no Magellan, but I'm a big fan. Magellan was killed in the Philippines; I would complete his work by continuing his round-the-world journey.

"Sorry about the terror alert," said Genghis, dropping me at the Manilla airport. "You'll get shaken down three or four times by security before they'll let you on the plane." He wasn't kidding.

It started just after I stepped off the curb into the terminal. Everything and everyone had to be funneled into a metal detector. It only took ten minutes. There was another one to access the ticket counter. Boarding pass in hand, I proceeded through the usual security channel, but it was much tighter than most. Everyone was not only x-rayed, but also got the pat-down treatment – very democratic, I thought. All the bags were opened and pilfered carefully by the checkers.

Downstairs, there was another metal detector to pass through to enter the boarding lounge. As the plane was boarding, there was a final round of bag-inspection. If Abu Sayyaf was busy trying to figure out how to penetrate this much security, they were not focusing on much lower-hanging fruit.

The flight went from Manilla to Bangkok. I switched planes and, of course, collected even more millirems of x-ray radiation in the process. It was very late when we landed in Delhi.

I awoke in the hotel early on Sunday morning. It was a beautiful day. I took a stroll and was pleased to see not one but two sacred cows wandering the streets near my hotel. I returned to my room, and thought about what I should do.

It wasn't that far to Agra and the Taj Mahal. The Taj Mahal! It's the Mona Lisa of architecture, among the most beautiful and vain-glorious constructs of history. I began to think I could do it. Therefore, I had to try. It would be a five hour bus ride, each way. That sounded grueling. I checked with my hotel manager. He recommended against. "If you need to be back in town tomorrow, then I would say you need to tell your company that you are sick and spend the night in Agra. It's a tough road."

Well, I couldn't do that. "How much for a car and driver?" I asked.

He raised his eyebrows. "My, you're determined. That would be a bit pricey." He gave me an estimate. I figured it would be worth it. He made the arrangement for me while I picked at breakfast.

The car arrived in a few minutes, and I wasted no time. "Thanks, see you this evening."

"Yeah, you say. Good luck!"

My driver didn't seem to be in a hurry. We were in heavy traffic, and he kept lugging the engine in third gear at low speeds. After a few minutes I risked it and asked him to speed up.

"Boss, I can't exceed speed limitations," he replied. Finally, we broke through traffic and entered the main road to Agra. It wasn't much of a road, and all of it was under construction. There were more jams and snarls. The blue sky of morning quickly turned dark as monsoon clouds built up. It was nearly noon. We were barely a third of the way.

The weather broke. The construction crews disappeared with the first fat rain drops. In fact, we'd traveled past zone of renovation, and with the workers disappearance, so went the asphalt. The road was now dirt and rapidly becoming mud. We slowed even more. Then my driver insisted on a break.

While I didn't support this decision, he was the driver. We strolled inside a roadside service center comprised of a single small building with a single person serving curry in disposable fast food bowls. We spent 30 minutes getting and eating food. I was relieved to get back in the car as it was almost 2pm. The rains were just getting started.

That's when the car wouldn't start. The driver was unconcerned and opened the hood (the "bonnet" as he called it). He fiddled for many minutes. I got out of my useless but dry spot in the back seat to see what he was up to. That's right, I made the command decision to be a micromanager.

I watched him fiddle with all the wrong things. He kept poking a screwdriver into the carburetor. "It's probably the condenser, points, or plugs," I informed him in what I thought was a helpful tone. For this, I earned a look of supreme contempt.

Still, my micromanagement did pay off, in that other drivers who'd stopped for food saw me peering into the engine compartment and came over to offer their advice. "You certainly won't fix it that way," one of them said. "Kindly give me that tool."

My driver did so. This helpful good Samaritan pulled the condenser, held it up into the rain, and declared, "Oh, yes, it's burned out."

To my amazement, he ran to his own car and pulled out a huge repair kit. The thing contained almost everything for any kind of automotive failure. He didn't have the right condenser, but by golly he put something in our engine that worked.

"Hurrah!"

We were all thrilled and thanked the man profusely. I tried to give him some rupees, which he absolutely would not accept.

It was now 4:30. "The Taj will close at 6:00pm." The rain was pounding in a manner that signaled "just getting' started." Visibility was poor, and the light was prematurely gloomy.

I'd seen the Mona Lisa. It's a nice work, not Da Vinci's finest endeavor in my humble estimation. "How long to the Taj?" I asked my driver.

"Oh, three, maybe four hours."

I did what I never like to do; I threw in the towel.

"Home, James." My driver nodded like he was familiar with this expression. We slogged our way toward Delhi. I got back to my hotel well after dinner, having missed the Taj Mahal but at least getting a taste of life in India.

That taste did not include supper, as everything was closed.

Moving the Needle

Best to know friend from foe.

Aberdeen Proving Ground was legendary, and I was now being waved through the security gate. What could be more cool?

I drove dusty roads following the signs that guided me to the Tank Proving Ground. That was where I'd been instructed to meet the other members of the commercial team working a big problem that my little company had been dragged into, by virtue of the fact that we supplied the digital compass.

When I thought of compasses before this job, I had two prominent images: one was a painting of Columbus, standing proudly astride the storm-blown prow of the Santa Maria, his primitive analog compass needle pointing due west. The other: my not much changed boy scout compass that fit in my pocket and helped me earn the Orienteering merit badge.

That was then and this was now. Our compasses were digital; they were calibrated to a high degree of accuracy which was preserved by active software compensation fed by other sensors. They adjusted for tilt, inclination, and smoothed out the bounce of austere roads. The vehicle this particular unit was strapped to was the U.S. Army Stryker – think of it as a twelve-ton tank bristling with machine guns, sensors, and swathed in thick armor to protect the valuable cargo of U.S. soldiers

This being 2006, American soldiers were battling two land wars in Asia. Robust systems and robust back-ups to those systems was the name of the game. To continue any level of public support for these wars, American casualties needed to be disproportionately low versus those of the adversary, at ratios the Pentagon Vietnam War planners of the previous century could only envy.

The Stryker was riddled with redundancy.

Our little digital compass was sort of an afterthought, but of critical value in the battlefield environment where GPS could be interrupted. The smoke and the fog of war could make eyeballing an escape route challenging, and no single point of failure could be countenanced. In the rush to deploy these vehicles and augment what had become the very vulnerable Humvee, our device had been tossed in. We were called to Aberdeen to help put our technology through its paces and prove the Army had chosen correctly. No pressure.

Our device was deployed upon was the NBC Stryker model. It's specialized purpose was to detect Nuclear, Biological, and Chemical war agents. The vendors of the Stryker's sensor package were all well-known, very large defense contractors. Our 20 person outfit was totally mismatched. Each of the three companies sent a representative.

We assembled in a logistics lobby and casually introduced ourselves to each other. We struck up a conversation. It turned out, the other two guys from big defense companies in Detroit and Louisiana knew each other well. It seemed they orbited together frequently as their sensor solutions were commonly packaged together for many makes and models of U.S. military hardware.

"Tony," said Roger, the rep from Louisiana, "you look like shit, man. Good to see you." Smiles all around. From my view, Tony looked pretty together.

"My boss canceled my vacation with a smile so's I could work with your sorry ass again on this one," quipped Tony. He had a thick British accent. I'm notoriously deficient in this area, but hazarded a guess.

"Tony, is that a Midlands accent?" I asked.

"Oh, fuck off, man," he laughed. "I'm from Manchester." He shook my hand warmly. "But I'm Motor-City thirty years now. I love it."

"Gentlemen," said a crisply starched private who'd entered the lobby. "Follow me."

We did, and strolled under the hot Maryland sun a few hundred meters to the "hangar." That's what the two security crew called it, anyway. It was a large dome-like structure with netting and camouflage liberally applied across its vast expanse. It was war-time, after all.

"Welcome to the hanger, gentlemen. I need your passports."

We dumped our three blue booklets on the desk in front of the two guys, one of whom came around and started wanding us. "Put your computer bags over there," he said. A third man entered from behind the desk and begin gingerly rifling through the bags.

"Jenkins," said the seated man. "Where are you from?"

"California."

He nodded, and politely handed me back my passport. He repeated the process for Roger. The last one was Tony.

"Nottingham," he said. "Where are you from?"

"Detroit."

"I'm sorry," said the man, suddenly standing erect. "What did you say? Did you say Detroit?"

"That's right, chap, Detroit, Michigan," said Tony, quite affably, too.

"What did you just call me?"

"Chap?" said Tony. "I think."

"You said you're from Detroit. What kind of accent is that?"

"Hey," said Roger, "hold up there. Tony's been working with me for nearly fifteen years."

The security officer pivoted harshly to face Roger. "Was I addressing you? Please stand quiet. Over there." He pointed to the far wall of the room. "Same for you." Roger and I did as instructed.

The man turned back to Tony. "I want to know where you're from."

"Ah, certainly, yes, I'm from Detroit. Born in the U.K."

"So you're a foreigner?"

"Sir," pleaded Tony, "I've been working in this country all my adult life. You've studied my passport. I'm American as you."

"You're not," said the officer clearly taking offense. "I need to make a phone call. Go stand over there with the others."

When he'd left the room to make his call, Roger summed it up. "This is a shit-fest. Sorry, old chap."

"What the fuck," said Tony under his breath. "We're fucking lead NATO members together."

The security man came back after a few minutes. "Gentlemen, you're all cleared to work on the Stryker today. I've detailed a personal security watch on this guy…Nottingham. We'll be watching you closely."

Tony was just too damn smart to say anything, at least not until we were all out at the tarmac, watching the Stryker roar through its paces.

"Well, gents, guess you must fucking feel good about all this then; got your 'Don't Tread on Me' all turned on us poor Brit minorities."

"Oh come on, Tony," said Roger. "Deal with it. We've got young, over-eager kids in uniform, just like you."

Tony sighed. "Another two years to retirement, so I'll let you slide, fucking comparing Lord Mountbatten to George Bush junior in his fake Air National Guard days." That was a lot to unpack.

All systems passed the test that day. In celebration, the three of us overpaid contractors had a steak dinner together, and spent most of it drinking Beefeater on the rocks and insulting each other's nations.

You can't really get paid for a better time.

YAKIMA TRAINING CENTER, WASHINGTON – 2006

Tank Warfare

Always wear your helmet.

Although a fan of Rommel vs. Monty on the deserts of North Africa, I knew immediately I wasn't cut out for tank warfare. The helmet I wore was saving my life multiple times. Without it, I would have been killed instantly. That's how hard my head hit the steel insides of the tank, technically a massively up-armored troop transport. The crew lead who sat across the troop compartment from me, in his dark glasses and in the same Kevlar helmet I wore, watched me closely. His face gave away nothing. He said nothing.

As there was no damage, I tried to turn my attention back to my notebook computer.

"Missed that last reading," said the driver up in front over the PA. That's because I'd been momentarily stunned by impact and forgotten what I was there to do. I compelled my eyes to refocus on the running string of numbers on my screen.

"308.5 degrees," I shouted. "309.3.   310.1.   308.3…." I fell back into routine, shouting out the directional headings recorded by my company's digital compass, mounted atop the vehicle as it sped over an austere unpaved section of trail, deep in the heart of Yakima Army Test Grounds. It went on like this for a while, until the Stryker hit some kind of divot in the road, and I plunged toward the right side wall, my helmet making a solid "dong!" as my head hit a steel support joist. This time, although the computer had nearly slipped away from me, I recovered quickly and did not miss a reading. "312.1 degrees. 311.4…."

I stole a glance across the cabin to my military escort. My vision crossed the filtering clouds of Yakima dust roiling inside. He had one hand casually on a support strap, but otherwise seemed very comfortable with the ride. I smiled and gave him a thumbs up. To my surprise, his mouth curled up ever so slightly. Essentially, the first acknowledgement of my existence the whole afternoon.

"Going up a rise," came the driver's voice. "Then we'll do some 360s per the test plan. You OK in back." It was not so much a question as a command.

"Great," I informed him. The 360s were jagged, jolting, and nausea-inducing. Thankfully, I wasn't required to take any reading until we came out of them. By that time, I was struggling to quell a rising tide that threatened to power up through my esophagus. My susceptibility to motion sickness in an enclosed land vehicle with no view of the outside world is only exceeded by my inclination to vomit shortly after boarding any kind of small sea craft. For reasons I can't explain, massive turbulence in the air doesn't bother me in the least. The little bag in every seat back pocket is to me just a convenient place to sketch out notes when the seat-belt sign prevents me from getting up to forage for my notebook.

Now I felt the need to expel lunch in a very compelling, projectile-vomit kind of way. Now some people are afraid to barf; not me. I've done it more than enough times to know that it's really a lot more comfortable to upchuck than to withhold. In this instance, however, I was reticent to soil the insides of a multi-million dollar piece of government hardware. Especially when I was here to do a job. I fought the urge.

The driver straightened out and began to plow downhill. That was my cue. I resumed reading out the compass headings flickering onto my PC screen at ten second intervals.

"181.3 degrees. 180.9. 180.3. 179.8." I let the symmetry of the numbers, which were indeed very good news for our purposes in this evaluation, soothe my roiling gut. The long drive in a straight line continued for many minutes. The compass was remarkably rock-solid.

The nausea slowly passed and so did the compass. After a further ten minutes, the Stryker came to a halt, and devils of white dust piled in upon us.

"Looks like we're all good," came the driver's voice. "Thanks for your effort. We're gonna take a break and then test some other systems. You're all done here."

That came as mixed news, because the queasiness wasn't entirely gone, and now I had to clamber back out of this monstrosity. Somehow, I did, though at the end I had to jump what was for me a very uncomfortable distance to get back on solid ground.

Instead, I found a firm handhold and slid myself off. My boots touched ground, and I was rocked with a wave of relief.

I turned away from the vehicle, looked at the desert and purple mountains on the horizon. I'd done it. I was so relieved that I decided to go ahead and project out, away from the vehicle. It came in three big heaves. It felt really, really good. I wiped my mouth with the back of my hand.

My military escort hopped down easily next to me. "Hey, great job. Most of the techs vomit inside. Thanks for saving me from clean-up duty."

Now that was high praise. Maybe I *was* cut-out for tank warfare after all.

Stryker armored troop transport

YANTAI, CHINA – 2007

Sibling Rivalry

Gary and I spent entirely too much time together and we crossed a line. Some would call it the DMZ.

"You know," said Gary, "Your President Bush is crazy. He's starting wars for no reason."

Gary was Chinese, and readers by now probably know I'm from California. He was my main sales representative for the nation of China, where 40% of my business was. Of course, 100% of his business was with my company. We really ought not be talking politics, but we couldn't help ourselves. Talking politics and history would be my full time job if I could earn a living from it. I suspect for Gary it would be a similar story.

I took my time with the riposte to Gary's bold statement. While he was absolutely right – George W. Bush had invaded Iraq for reasons that proved to be falsehoods – it was part of the game we played to take well-targeted jabs at the other's government. Simply agreeing with him would be a disappointment for us both. No, this was an opportunity.

We needed this kind of opportunity to while

227

away the vast hours of windshield time we shared together on these trips. On this one, we drove through three provinces along the Yangtze River, and stayed night after night in the AnTing Villa, China's answer to America's dismal Motel 6. Plus, we were on the final leg, after a quick jump to Shandong Province, rapidly approaching the Yantai Airport, where I would catch a flight to Japan. There wouldn't be another opportunity for a solid political romp with Gary for another three months.

It was, therefore, critical that the "ball be kept in play" with what I said next.

"You know, Gary," I said, "being the sole remaining superpower burdens the United States with an excessive level of responsibility. China should really step up and contribute."

"You think we would have attacked Iraq?" he questioned. "No, we never would."

"A military response is not the only way to step up as the world's next superpower, you know."

Gary had been staring full ahead, both hands on wheel. Now he turned to me with wide eyes behind his thick lensed glasses.

"Uhm," I said. "Road."

He turned his gaze back to the highway and cut the curve only a little sloppily. "China has no interest in being a superpower," he said.

"That's too bad," I informed him. "Because China has no choice in the matter." I immediately regretted the statement as Gary diverted his gaze back to me.

"Kai che," I suggested. "Drive."

He did, but Gary was agitated. He said nothing as the car crested a long low rise. Below us appeared the town of Yantai, a frontier city bordered by the Gulf of China, beyond whose blue-green waters lay the Korean peninsula.

"If war happens with the United States," said Gary, "You know we could defeat you easily."

Now we were getting somewhere. "Nope. You could not."

"We could," he said with great assurance. "We have already defeated the United States in one war."

I had to think about this. It was a trick assertion. We'd been allies in the second world war, but Americans and Chinese had killed each other in the Korean War. There'd been another war after that one, but it was even more complex for the U.S.-China rivalry.

"Not yet, you haven't. You haven't beat us yet."

The car became very quiet. Gary and I are both students of history.

"Hmph," he said. We slowly approached the Yantai airport, our point of separation. "Hmph," he repeated.

"You know that war is not over," I said. I knew he knew that and was stewing in it. "No peace treaty has been signed. North and South Korea are still in a technical state of war, after five decades. You haven't won yet."

"Tim, you are denying the obvious," Gary said. "We've won the war, all except the official peace treaty."

"So you're saying that's it? No more hostilities will occur as a result of the Korean War?"

We were pulling up toward the airport terminal. Gary said nothing. Air China and Shandong Airline marked jetliners lined the near side of the airfield. On the far side of the field was a line of Chinese built Russian MIG-21 Floggers – combat fighter jets. Yantai was then a "mixed-use" field – hosting both commercial and military aircraft. The MIGs were clearly positioned to be, what I had learned in the defense business, were called continental defense fighters.

"What's with the MIGs?" I asked. "Who are those for? Japan?"

"You know better," Gary responded quickly. "We must defend against Kim Jong Il. He is developing nuclear bombs." Gary's reputed victorious surrogate state now threatened China with nuclear devastation. I watched him furrow his brow.

He pulled the car to the curb. "Great trip, Gary," I said.

"It's very good," he responded. He smiled gracefully. We shook hands, then hugged. As I walked into the terminal, I was glad he'd never mentioned the other war.

Vietnam. That would keep us yakking on our next trip.

GREENSBORO, NORTH CAROLINA – 2014

Unintentional Gandhi Mode

Gandhi traveled light, but would he have approved of this?

The integration of our new company was about to begin, but for our two product lines to meld, there was still much to be done. Although the official merger wouldn't happen until January 1ˢᵗ, the new boss had asked Blaze, Terry, and me to come to North Carolina two weeks before Christmas. She suggested the Courtyard Marriott, Greensboro.

As always, Blaze and I made separate travel arrangements. At his request, I booked Terry's hotel room. We were set.

All three of us were ticketed on the same flight into Raleigh. It worked out fine. I got the rental car and we drove about an hour through the deep winter darkness to Greensboro. Arriving so late in a new town, we decided not to risk starvation, and grabbed a huge sack of burgers and fries at a McDonalds on the way. When business calls, flexibility and sacrifice are expected. Blaze, who normally practices veganism, was so hungry that he tore open the bag and started handing out Quarter Pounders with Cheese. He did more than his fair share to reduce the burger count.

We drove on at high speed. I'd fortunately asked for extra napkins as the Big Mac sauce from my sandwich dripped onto the steering wheel. There was no slowing us down until we arrived at the Courtyard by Marriott, Greensboro, just about midnight. We piled into the lobby.

"Seems kind of far away from the office," Terry noted, looking at the map application on his iPhone.

"Only ten minutes straight down the freeway," I assured him. But that didn't sound right. We were supposed to be next door to the new headquarters.

"I have your reservation," said the efficient hotel clerk, pointing to Terry. "Not yours," she pointed at Blaze, "and not yours either." She pointed at me.

"Hmm. Is there another Courtyard in town?"

"Y'all know we got three hotels right here in Greensboro," she pointed out.

She quickly called the other two. "You," she pointed at Blaze, "are at the facility just north of us." She pointed at me. "Right now, sir, you're nowhere."

"Any chance you can just re-book us all at this one?" I pointed to the printout of my boss's email, the one adjacent to our new headquarters.

She worked the phones. It was a non-trivial request. "That's right," she said into the receiver wedged between her shoulder and ear, "Three gentlemen, booked three different ways." Somehow, she got all the ducks in a row for us in just about five minutes.

"All set," she said. "Now you all go straight to that hotel and don't get lost."

She seemed to have this motley crew well figured out. "It's getting too late for more adventures," said Blaze. "But we'll try!"

Just a few minutes later, we were there – our home for the next few nights. "Ok," said the clerk, "here's your key," for Terry. "Here's your key," for Blaze. "I'm sorry, honey, what's your name again?"

"Jenkins."

"Wait a minute," she said. "This is North Carolina, you say Jenkins you might as well say Smith. We got a lot of Jenkins tonight."

I dug out my ID and handed it to her.

"You got two reservations here," she said. "Hold on." She worked the computer keyboard. "OK, ya'll set." She handed me an electronic room key. Home at last!

The next morning, because the merger wasn't official yet, we met in a conference room inside the hotel rather than in the sprawling headquarters next door. The sessions were productive, and the team worked well together. We were all in the same business selling similar products, so maybe that's why. Part of it was just that teamwork is a spontaneous evolutionary human characteristic. We were having a lot of fun.

Late on the third day, we retreated to wash up before the big team dinner. I brushed my teeth, changed into more casual wear, and noted that my bed was still an unmade mess; huh, no maid service the entire stay. It wasn't so bad as no clean-up was an excellent reminder that being a slob was not really permissible at home, so why should it be on the road?

After a fabulous dinner bonding with the new team, we returned to the hotel to grab our bags and check out. Blaze and Terry paid their bills, and stepped outside to gather in the cool evening air as I handed my keycard to the clerk.

"What room?"

"314."

"Nope, you're all set. Please stay with us again."

"Can I get a receipt?"

"No charge," she said. "You never checked in."

"I stayed three nights in that room!" I protested.

"Nope," she said. "Not in the system. No charge."

"How is that possible?" No maid service! She didn't know I existed.

The clerk laughed. "This key is blank. Room 314 hasn't been rented in a week. You were just sleeping there. Didn't anyone walk in on you? They could have. Sorry." She grinned. "Please stay with us next time."

I did. I sort of felt obligated.

MISSION MODE

HONSHU, JAPAN – 2008

The Fixers

Those who can fix, fix.

There was not a thing broken that Mike couldn't fix. He was that good.

Mike had a range of talents – he could weld, solder, build, requisition, carve, program, de-louse, lay masonry, perform higher math functions, manage suppliers, follow Generally Approved Accounting Principles, and almost anything else you might ever need done in a company. He'd built his own house, home-schooled his kids, and made a tidy sum in his last job, at a software start-up.

He didn't travel much -- never had much need.

That changed when he joined our little start-up company. We had very sophisticated customers around the world. Mike was not the sort of guy who aspired to work with customers. "Who the fuck has patience for customers?" he would proclaim in his Brooklyn accent. "They tend to just get in my way."

It was true. We mostly kept him away from customers, but one day a certain critical customer in Japan had a problem with their test gear – not our test gear, mind you – but complex radio frequency equipment, long since out of warranty, that was nonetheless needed for the customer to test our products. And so it was that we happily agreed to send Mike to Japan to take a look and remedy the situation.

When informed of our decision, Mike stood up from his workbench in the lab, and said "I need to pack and tell my wife. She's gonna bitch like no tomorrow."

"Mike," reasoned Blaze, "you absolutely don't have to go. It was just an idea."

"What? No, I'll go. Happy to get out of the house. What time is my flight?" he glanced at his watch.

"Can you leave tomorrow?" I asked. "It would be great to get you out there ASAP."

Mike looked confused. He scratched his wavy brown hair. "Tomorrow? For Chrissakes, I'm busy here. If we're talking about tomorrow let me focus on this shit. PLEASE," and he sat back at his bench.

Blaze and I performed a silent, invisible 'high-five' with just our eyes, and I quickly booked a ticket. All the arrangements were coordinated with the customer that evening, who would send a driver to pick Mike up at Narita Airport, bring him to the customer site, install him at a nearby hotel, and get the hell out of his way so he could fix the dang thing.

After exiting customs, Mike strolled into a crowded reception parlor with many folks holding signs with names. He quickly spotted his: a meticulously suited young man held a sign that said, "Mike Miller." The young man helped him with his roller bag, ushered him into the back seat of a limo, and drove him several hours into the far northern suburbs of Tokyo. As it was nearly 8pm, he was delivered to his hotel, and checked in.

Two of the customer's managers greeted him in the hotel lobby with deep bows. After check-in, they took him to a fabulous traditional dinner of sushi, yakitori, various delicacies, the likes of which Mike had never seen. He was a good sport, and after dropping his chopsticks a few times, was given a fork.

"The rice and teriyaki chicken were great," he later reported. "The beer was even better. I didn't care for the saké. They kind of made me mad, every time I emptied my saké glass they just refilled it."

The next morning, his driver returned and brought him to the customer facility. The same two managers, dressed in their immaculate blue suits, gave him a bow, and escorted him to the broken machine.

Mike studied it closely. It filled most of the room. Very clearly, it used some kind of microwave generation and amplified heat to produce a petrochemical residue of exceeding purity. "Mike-san," said one of the customers, "no more dripping chemicals; can you fix?"

Mike scratched the brown curls. "Well, fuck me," he said. The customers, whose English was very limited, both smiled. They backed away as instructed and let the expert tackle the problem.

"I had no clue what this machine was," said Mike, later. "It had nothing to do with our product. There wasn't a radio frequency integrated circuit anywhere in sight. By this time, I figured, wrong company but I went to work anyway."

Mike traced the electrical, the pneumatic, coolant, and hydraulic lines; then he sketched the reactor, the liquid drains; thermal venting and gas relief system. Then he cracked open the tool kits and began diddling. They made him stop for a bento-box lunch, of which he consumed the rice and chicken teriyaki. "Kind of pissed me off, they didn't serve any beer." After lunch, he found a blown winding of some sort; smoked by excessive current.

One of the customer technicians brought him a spare, which he replaced. Then they fired it up. Drip, drip, drip....

"They had a huge party for me that night," said Mike. "I thought that was a good time to tell them I had come to the wrong company, and needed to go fix my real customer's problem."

He needn't have worried.

The other Mike Miller had been dashed to OUR customer site. He recognized nothing of our radio frequency testing realm, but quickly found a blown tube from the days pre-dating transistors. He jury-rigged a modern replacement, and our customer, too, was back in business. Mike didn't know this, and protested when his driver put him back at Narita airport. He called Blaze.

"What the fuck, man? There were apparently two Mike Millers, and I went to the wrong company. Now I need to get onsite at our real customer."

"What are you talking about, you did great!" said Blaze. "Get on the plane, come on home. You're a hero!" People who just know how to fix things can, apparently, fix anything, and everything.

Both Mike Millers were heroes. It's a shame they never met. I like to think maybe they will on some future trouble call.

TAIWAN – 2008

That Dog Don't Hunt Fair

Bloodhounds are natural born hunters -- don't let size fool you.

It would be hard to use the term "hamburger" on the sandwiches we'd been given on the flight to Taipei. Wrapped in clear plastic, the bun looked very fresh and reminded me of the outstanding, soft, semi-sweet rolls I'd enjoyed at little bakeries throughout Taiwan. The meat certainly wasn't hamburger; it looked a little more like Spam. Still, this kind of Taiwanese-style burger was generally fresh and flavorful.

Arriving late at night, Dave and I both hoarded our sandwiches for a little late night nosh at the hotel in place of dinner.

We came off the plane and rolled our bags past duty-free liquor and tobacco shops, most of which were closed or closing for the night. We breezed through short lines at immigration and aimed our roller bags for the final hurdle, Taiwan customs, just 50 meters ahead.

Between us and a quick airport exit stood a young woman in a white, military-style uniform. She wore a white hat with dark brim, much like a British meter maid's hat. In her hand was a silvery leash, and at the end of the leash was a beagle

It was an official Taiwanese Customs Frontier inspection beagle. It was a tiny creature also decked in white and wearing an identical little meter maid hat on its head. It ranks among the cutest dogs I've ever seen. Dave couldn't resist petting it. The little guy's handler let him pick it up, and she looked on, smiling, as Dave bonded with this pint-sized canine welcome committee.

The dog was wagging its tail and obviously happy for the attention. It sniffed Dave, and seemed to like what it smelled. It kept trying to crawl further up his shoulder. Its little paws began to scrabble at the backpack slung over Dave's shoulder.

That's when the dog's handler asked Dave to set the backpack down and open it up. He set the beagle down first, then the backpack, and unzipped the top pocket.

The beagle jumped and nearly disappeared inside.

"Are you carrying any meat?" the woman asked Dave.

"Meat? Oh, I've got an airline sandwich."

"Can you remove it?" she asked. That was hardly necessary as the beagle retreated from the backpack with the little burger firmly in its teeth.

"I'm sorry, sir, you'll have to throw it away." Dave extracted the sandwich from the dog's grasp. He looked surprised and disappointed.

"Really? That was going to be dinner." In hindsight, we could have probably ripped open the sandwiches and wolfed them down right there in front of the Frontier dog. That would have felt petty, though, and it was just doing its job, after all.

We surrendered our sandwiches reluctantly. The woman took them to a nearby trash can and disposed of them. Dave looked at her, then at me, then at the beagle. He wasn't wagging his tail anymore. His little beagle eyes looked as sad as Dave's.

Seems it's a tough life in the Taiwan Customs Canine Core.

QINGDAO, CHINA – 2008

Crossing Shandong

Leave no customer behind.

We'd no sooner walked in the door when a text came in on Blaze's phone.

"Oh, good news," he said. "Hisense wants to see us too." Hisense is the General Electric of China! Good news, except for the fact that they are headquartered in Qingdao.

"Dude," I told him, "if you think that's good news, then this isn't Yantai. This is Wei Hai, and so are you." We'd laughed earlier that morning at the road sign for a nearby town that was pronounced "way high." Blaze had actually been there a few years previously. "Qingdao is on the opposite side of the peninsula, and our itinerary is packed."

"It would be great if we could grant their wish," he smiled.

Damn. It sure would be. We stood in another customer's lab while their engineers tuned their circuit with our chip onboard. Across the room I could see a big map centered on Beijing, but with vast detail on our present whereabouts and circumstance.

We left the engineers and strolled over to it. I pointed out the problem to Blaze. "We're on the north coast. Qingdao is over these mountains on the south coast.

"Is that a road?" he asked.

"That squiggly line?" I said. "Could be."

"It's drivable," said Helen, our host for this customer. "It will take you four hours. You want to go to Qingdao? It's not an easy ride."

"I do," I volunteered. "How much for a taxi?"

She laughed. "I'll order one, and tell him it's a flat fee." It turned out to be a bargain at 500 yuan.

The delicious dumpling lunch we'd had last time we were here was left to Blaze, Helen, and the customer engineers. The taxi screeched to a halt in front of their lobby at 11:58am. "Tell Hisense I'll be there at 4pm. Catch up with you in Shanghai."

"Hasta la vista!" said Blaze, smiling.

Helen shouted some instructions to my driver. I heard the words "kuài yì diǎn!" so my driver knew I was in a hurry. "B-bye!" she said. The driver tore out of the parking lot. We sailed onto a freshly asphalted highway that rose into the mountains, then quickly became a narrow, two-lane road loaded with hairpin curves and slow-moving trucks. The driver cursed and shouted at them, until he smilingly found a way to pass.

I'd done this before in China. None of it got me too excited. I was more worried about making that 4:00 o'clock appointment. I did ask the driver to pull over at one point so I could join him in the front seat. That's because no backseat of any cab you'll ever take in China has a functional seatbelt.

At a small, dusty roadside intersection at the top of the mountain, the driver pulled into the parking lot of a little store. He apologized for the delay and ran inside. Two minutes later he was back. "Eat?" he said in Chinese.

He opened a multi-bladed knife that dangled from his keychain and cut open the plastic, revealing six sausages. It was definitely not Oscar Meyer. He squeezed the plastic and one of the sausages started to emerge, along with drops of semi-translucent grease. "You eat," he said. I wasn't going to argue. The sausage was cold and the taste was vaguely metallic. I ate my share and didn't complain. It beat the heck out of not eating.

At the base of the mountains, now on the southern side of the peninsula, the road again widened into a modern superhighway – with a difference. In the distance, I could see a toll gate. The driver started cursing.

"No problem," I said, and tried to hand him money.

"No, no, we don't pay," he replied. Suddenly we were off-roading into the weeds. The ride was incredibly rough. We moved at a snail's pace to avoid breaking an axle. It took nearly twenty minutes of sneaking through tall grasses, plunging in and out of chuck-holes, and making a few backtracks when our progress was blocked by gullies. At last, we were two hundred meters past the toll gate and snuck back onto the highway. The driver was grinning and gave a thumbs up as we bounced back onto the asphalt and accelerated away.

At 3:48 we entered the city limits of Qingdao. That cabbie was a total ace and went directly into the downtown of the famous beer-quaffing coastal city full of high-rises. Hisense owned one of them, and he dropped me in front of the lobby at 3:57.

I entered, dusted the shoulders of my jacket, and was greeted by my escort as she came off the elevator to fetch me. An hour later, we completed our discussion, and the largest electronics conglomerate in China was now securely in our portfolio.

Needless to say, I had tipped the driver well. And that night, I tipped a Qingdao beer on draft, straight from the source.

SHENZHEN, CHINA – 2009

Out-Foxing The Giant

They played hard-ball. We gave as good as we got.

"Look out for the forklift!"

The damn thing skidded away from us at the last possible second. The driver gave us a dirty look as he sped away with his huge pallet of boxes.

"Sorry about that," said Wilton. "This place is crazy. Complete chaos. They won't stop for anything, it's like walking in the middle of the street in Manhattan."

Wilton was our rep based in nearby Hong Kong. We continued unescorted across the giant campus. It was a different world. Over 100,000 workers were feverishly building much of the world's consumer electronics goods right here.

Minutes before, we'd checked in to the security desk. A team of three people looked us over and photocopied our passports. We shifted uncomfortably, awaiting their determination that we might enter to meet with our customer. The process was slow. I had to switch my heavy computer bag from one shoulder to the other, more than once.

247

At last, with just a silent, grudging nod of the head, we were allowed inside the bustling complex. We finished the journey across the dangerous, unmarked forklift highway and entered our appointed building, found the conference room, and set up.

The customer walked in two minutes later. "Hello," she said. "Welcome to Out-Fox Electronics." We knew her by email and phone, but this was our first meeting. We made small-talk. "OK," she said, "shall we start?"

"Sure," I said, pulling the laptop out of my bag. "Do you have a cable for that projector?" I pointed to a huge white screen on the far wall, but saw something was wrong.

Our customer stared at what I'd laid on the table. "You brought a computer inside the facility?"

"We just have a few slides," interjected Wilton. "Tim would like to help give you a better picture ..."

"Oh, no, this is terrible," she said.

"Huh?" asked Wilton. "Pardon me, is there a problem?"

Her lips were pursed with concern. She looked around the room uncomfortably. "No, I'm so sorry, no foreigners are allowed to bring a computer on the premises of Out-Fox Electronics. Didn't security ask you to check your computers at the desk?"

"Nope," I said.

"OK," she punched a number into her phone. "Just wait, please." She explained the situation to somebody, and within two minutes five security folks entered the room. Without asking, they began scooping up my computer and laptop bag. They hesitated briefly, asked Wilton a question, and then grabbed his as well.

I smelled disaster in the air. Not only were they going to confiscate our machines, they were going to ruin our meeting – a critical negotiation for which I'd flown six thousand miles. I couldn't let that happen.

"Follow us," one of the security folks said.

"One moment, please," I said in Chinese. I reached for my bag, but he wasn't letting go, so I unzipped it while he held it, and pulled out a document the size of a ream of paper. It was – Out-Fox Electronics' terms and conditions of purchase, that I had red-lined on the flight over the Pacific, at least up to a certain point.

"Sir, you must go with security now," the customer said.

"Of course, so let me first give this to you," I slid the document across the desk, "just to let you know that we cannot sign your contract." I reached back into the bag, still in security's grip, and grabbed a single sheet of paper. "We'll need you to sign our terms and conditions of sale, which should be no problem for you. As you can see it's very simple."

The poor woman looked mortified. She was taking glares from the security folks. I slid the single sheet across the table to her. "Ok," I said, "we're off to security. Please let me know if you have any questions." Security now more or less pushed us toward the door. I paused briefly at the threshold, and said "Thank you for your time. Oh, and note, we can't sell you any product without your signature on that." I waved.

"Tim," said Wilton, "that was very impressive, but I'm not sure it will work."

"Yes it will," I told him. Out-Fox's customer, a world-famous brand name in communications, had been working with our company's designer for two years. Together, they had integrated our chip into the customer's product. There were no alternate solutions without a total redesign. "They might hate us for it, but they don't have a choice."

We arrived at the security office, and Out-Fox began exacting its vengeance. I watched them crack open my laptop, then they demanded the password, which I reluctantly typed in for them. They then proceeded to probe, dust, and prod my machine. After a long time they gave Wilton's a much more gentle inquisition. The lead IT security investigator was careful to glare at me harshly every few minutes.

After nearly an hour, it looked like they might be wrapping it up.

"Hey, Wilton," I asked, "any theory why they didn't just ask us if we had computers in our *computer* bags?"

He laughed. "Yes, I have a theory. They are so familiar with their way of doing things, they assume everyone else must be as well. A bit arrogant."

Just a year later Out-Fox became big news when numerous of their employees committed suicide from overwork and poor living conditions. Their largest customer began taking a very hard look at the situation. Said large customer was headed by a well-known genius who mostly wore a black long-sleeve turtleneck and blue jeans.

Out-Fox had to learn a little humility. Meantime, they signed our simple contract and we sold them millions and millions of chips.

Ticket to Suzhou

Buying the ticket was easy; not so getting on the train.

Suzhou is one of the best preserved ancient cities in China. Like Amsterdam, it's laid out on canals. It's only a 70 minute high-speed train ride from Shanghai. Having finished up my customer visits on Saturday evening, I planned a leisurely day-trip to Suzhou for Sunday morning.

The weather was great, and Shanghai was in full weekend bustle as I walked toward Hongqiao Station, which is the giant nexus for rail travel throughout China. The crowds thickened as I tried to work my way up the grand stairway leading into the station atrium and ticketing hall. It seemed unusually busy.

It was a full thirty-minute wait to get to the ticket counter. "One ticket for Suzhou," I told the agent.

"No tickets until 18:30 train," he said. 6:30pm, and it was only 10am now.

"Are you sure? No earlier trains?"

"Sold out. Today is a holiday."

Well, crud. My thoughts flashed to my last trip to Stockholm. I'd been there six or seven times, selling to Ericsson. On my final trip, my boss had joined me and suggested we go visit the wreck of the Vasa, a well-preserved ship scuttled long ago in Stockholm harbor. I passed, figuring I could focus on some prep work for upcoming meetings, and catch the Vasa on the next trip. "You know, that's a dangerous thought process," my boss had said. "You never know for sure about the next trip." He'd been right. A few months later I changed jobs, and haven't been back to Stockholm since.

I needed to get to Suzhou today. "OK," I told the ticket agent, and bought the late-day ticket.

Stepping out of the ticket hall, I watched as folks charged toward the train platforms. On the big departure board, I could see trains leaving for Suzhou every 30 minutes. My train was seven hours in the future.

I had to try to get on an earlier train. Platform 13 had one leaving in 11 minutes, and I headed there.

The throngs clustered and slowed as we approached the ticket checkers guarding the entrance to the platform. There were at least six of them, spread in a line. They seemed to give each ticket a cursory glance, then punched it.

After two minutes, an older checker glanced at my ticket and almost punched it. Then she saw her error. "Not this train, please wait." I smiled and thanked her, playing dumb, then slunk away.

Well, that hadn't worked.

There were many people and many more checkers, so I drifted to the back of the line and let the crowds push me toward another checker. It was the same story. He put his ticket clicker on the yellow paper, but caught himself. "You must wait for later train." OK.

Again, I milled toward the back of the throngs, which were still swelling. It was four minutes to departure. I kept my head low and aimed for yet another checker. This one seemed particularly busy, processing tickets very fast, and answering questions from passengers and other checkers.

She looked up at me and clicked my ticket. I think she must have recognized her mistake as she gave the ticket a final inspection for a fleeting second. Nonetheless, she handed it back.

I thanked her. I was going to Suzhou!

Now to find some unobtrusive standing room somewhere on the train. I lodged myself, along with about eight others, between two cars. A young lady, likely a college student, thoughtfully moved her Doraemon backpack to make room for me. The character on her backpack is best described as "a robotic cat who abhors violence," a beloved Japanese cartoon hero.

The train started rolling. It was very fast, but it soon decelerated for the first of what the electronic board in each car indicated would be several stops between Shanghai and Suzhou.

The train resumed its high-speed run between stops. In the next car, I saw a uniformed train official enter and begin inspecting the tickets of those seated. The Doraemon girl next to me saw her, too. She picked up her bag, and scuttled into the next car, away from the rail official. As the uniformed agent came close to entering my inter-car stow-away space, I followed suit. I went through four cars, until I saw the same girl. We exchanged smiles. Behind her was an open window onto the tracks. There were no more cars to run through.

The train made two more stops. There was one more before Suzhou. The train official entered our car. This wasn't looking good.

About 12 of us were bunched here in the end of the train. Some had legitimate tickets, but I knew of at least two who didn't. As the train lurched into its final stop before Suzhou, the train official threw open the door. She chose her first victim.

"You're on the wrong train," she said loudly, "get off!" The teenaged boy sullenly picked up his bag and jumped onto the platform. The agent checked another ticket. That one was ok. Then another. "You too! Get off!" That person was also forced to jump.

The train made a pre-departure intonation (call it a digital horn-blow). The agent looked at me. "Your ticket please." I smiled, and began fishing it out of my shirt pocket. It seemed to be a little sticky, but emerged at last, and I handed it over.

She glared at it. "This is the wrong—"

The doors closed with a steam compression noise. She looked at me again. I pointed out that my ticket said "Suzhou." The train began to roll.

"OK," she said. It wasn't ok, but it was too late.

The Doraemon girl and I had evaded ejection by mere seconds. We exchanged a thumbs-up.

Suzhou was gorgeous, and I made the most of those extra hours walking its ancient streets and floating on its grand canals.

CHANGSHU, CHINA – 2014

The Shortcut Home

Real-life action heroes can appear out of nowhere.

Our van was making good time coming back along the wide, modern superhighway whence it had come early that morning. We were now on the approaches to Shanghai, perhaps the greatest city in the early 21ˢᵗ century. It was an unusually, fabulously clear spring day, and we could now see that the gray wall ahead was resolving into the many hundreds of skyscrapers that make this city the most populous and cosmopolitan in China. Yet it was still 60 kilometers ahead.

The ultra-modern highway through Changshu was six lanes in each direction. The other reason it was so swiftly moving – aside from having not a single pothole or bump – was that there were very few entrances or exits. A vehicle that missed its off ramp would have to travel a farther 10 to 12 kilometers to find the next one. There were, however, periodic widenings of the shoulder that permitted vehicles to stop far away from traffic. They were spartan rest stops that even included a few porta potties, minimizing the risk that drivers might distract traffic by taking care of business on the side of the road.

The entire super-road was enclosed on both sides by an enormously tall fence; three meters of concrete at the foot, atop which rode a further five meters of chain-link, upon which rested a delicate nest of barbed concertina wire – 30 feet all tolled. Pedestrians or bicyclists were unlikely to amble onto the highway; a further enhancement that aided the unhindered flow of traffic.

"It's good for me at the next one," said Jackie to our driver. Jackie was our applications engineer for Jiangsu province. He was in his young twenties, friendly, and extremely technical. Customers loved Jackie, and we loved him too.

"Good applications engineers walk around with hundred dollar bills streaming off their backs," was a popular phrase in the semiconductor business. Good guys like Jackie would walk up to the whiteboard and sketch out the solution customers were looking for; they'd get you designed-in while you, the sales guy, put your feet up on the customer's conference table and relaxed. Then commission money would roll in – to the sales guy. It was like plucking money off the apps engineer's back.

"Ok," said Jackie, "slow down. This one!"

The van moved into one of the rest stops in the highway and parked next to the row of porta potties.

"Jackie," I pointed out, "We're almost back. You sure you need to go that badly?" These potties were never pleasant, as we all knew. But when duty calls...

"No," he replied. "I live there." He pointed past the tall fence, and beyond that past a mountain of construction debris and rubble that exceeded the fence's height by many meters. Following his gesture well beyond that, perhaps a quarter mile, stood a few brand new mid-rise apartment buildings – maybe 40 stories tall.

"There's no access," I pointed out.

"Don't worry," said Jackie. His last name was Chen, but as you might imagine, we all called him, "Jackie Chan."

He jumped out of the van, and we all got out to stretch our legs. "Thank you," he said, shaking our hands. Then he slung his computer back over his white short-sleeve dress shirt, and began sprinting for that imposing fence.

At a dead run he jumped and was able to grip the top of the concrete. He then lifted himself up and like Spiderman scaled the chain link. The sight of it gave me altitude sickness. "Be careful!" I shouted in Chinese. To my chagrin, he interrupted his climb to wave back at us, then continued up.

He reached the concertina wire, and paused to pull his backpack off and sling it over the barbed coils of the concertina wire. Then he belly-crawled gingerly over the backpack and suddenly was on the other side, Spider-manning his way down the opposite side.

"Jesus," I muttered. The other guys in our contingent just smiled.

"Jackie knows how to do it," one said.

He certainly did. We watched him let go and drop behind the concrete on the far side. He was invisible for several minutes. Then we could see him clambering over the immense pile of rubble and construction wreckage; twisted girders and mountains of brick and other debris. He was easily forty feet up when he disappeared down the far-side. Then he was gone.

"Let's go," said one of the guys.

"No, wait," I said. "Let's make sure he's OK."

It took a few more minutes. Then, high up on one of the mid-rises in the distance, we saw a figure emerge onto the tiny balcony. It was wearing a white short-sleeve shirt.

A tiny figure, Jackie was waving at us from the 35th floor. He was home, safe.

To call that guy anything other than "Jackie Chan" just wouldn't be right.

OVER THE SEA OF JAPAN – 2015

A Bargain at $48 Per Gallon

When you need a refill you'll gladly pay it.

Having read this far, you may have observed that I have an aptitude for self-inflicted injury. I've run while carrying scissors and picked up really hot pans without bothering about an oven mitt. Each time I celebrate my near miss of earning a Darwin Award, I know better than to say it can't happen to me again. Instead, I try to evaluate all the angles of how I can do it better, and less painfully, next time.

This is especially true of travel logistics, with which I have a bizarre fascination. If I can pack a fifth customer meeting into a third city in one day, I'll tend to err on the side of trying to do just that. It can make for an exhausting itinerary.

By way of illustration, there was the trip I made to Japan and China – to make sales calls, and mitigate a crisis.

With great care, I aligned the details of the visit. I'd see three customers in Japan on Tuesday, then I'd catch a late flight to Hong Kong and skitter across the frontier to China before catching some sleep in

Shenzhen. Upon waking I'd be in front of multiple customers in southern China. Then I'd fly to Shanghai to meet a few customers we hadn't yet been able to crack open.

A very packed five days. The result was suboptimal. The last customer visit in Japan was the one in crisis, and they were visibly angry. Our product had subjected these poor fellows to what is politely called "a quality excursion." That means our product had drifted off the rail of our standard performance in a sneaky way that wasn't an actual failure of the specification. If you've ever stayed at a hotel that advertised 'Color TV' and the TV in your room was colorful in its static and inability to actually show you the poor programming it normally delivered, then you know all about quality excursions.

I fell on the sword provided by the dozen members of the Japanese customer's delegation, only to check my watch to see I had to run to catch my Hong Kong flight. I bolted for the door. Being literally chased down the street by the customer was just the beginning of the awfulness.

They kept chasing us as we ran down the street and waved wildly at every passing cab. Finally, a cabbie took mercy on us and stopped. Technically, only I had a flight and was urgently needed at the airport, but our in-country team would not be left behind. I could hardly blame them for that.

Of all the travel logistical challenges I've self-inflicted, this was easily in the top five for biggest sin of over-ambition. That feeling was confirmed once my late night flight from Tokyo to Hong Kong was airborne. It was a new low-cost carrier in the mold of Southwest Airlines, but minus the great sense of humor and serious attention to delivering you at least one peanut packet and one free beverage on every flight.

No, this airline was hell-bent on out-cheapening even the cheapest U.S. carrier. The lovely flight attendants smiled as they rolled the drink cart down the aisle. I was parched beyond measure after my narrow escape from our angry customer. Continuing my theme of shooting myself in the foot, I'd barely caught the flight due to my delay and had had no time to buy a bottle of water. It was nearly 11pm, and the last sip of water I'd had was at lunch.

Busy on my laptop, I looked up to realize the drink cart had passed me by. Passengers on all sides of me were either sleeping or guzzling water from plastic bottles they'd just received. I strolled forward to trouble the galley staff. "Could I get some water, please?" I asked a dapperly uniformed young woman.

"Sir," she said with a smile, "Water is 200 yen."

I was taken aback but produced my credit card immediately.

"Cash," she added.

Bear in mind that these little bottles of water every conscious person onboard was nursing like a martini contained approximately 5 fluid ounces (0.15 liters). Two hundred yen, about $1.90, was a true king's ransom for one good swig of water, which I would have happily surrendered in a heartbeat to quench the aching thirst I felt – if only I could.

I pushed Chinese renminbi and Hong Kong dollars at her, wads of them.

She was so very, very sorry. She truly was. I almost felt bad. "Sir, we only accept yen." She'd clearly delivered this horribly bad news to many others before me, and didn't hold with it herself. Dozens and dozens of the little water bottles were at her elbow, but she was powerless to assist me without the requisite cash-only fee in the correct currency.

I'd been on the run in the hot Tokyo weather for more than seven hours since my last sip of anything, sweating profusely in the June Tokyo heat. It was a level of thirst seldom experienced. Every option was on the table. I could grab three of those little bottles and be locked in the lavatory guzzling before she knew what had hit her. Thankfully, I hit on a less larcenous solution before doing anything too crazed. Otherwise, this story might have included my being taken into custody on landing.

"Hong Kong dollars!" I called out, strolling back down the aisle toward my seat. "Who needs HKD? I accept Japanese yen only, please." Some of the passengers turned away in embarrassment, some laughed, but several reached for their cash. I had multiple offers in no time. The first one was a kind woman who knew what I really needed.

"Here, I have too many coins anyway," she said, absolutely refusing to accept any HKD in return. I thanked her profusely and told the others I'd be right back to convert their currency, as promised. First, I went back to the galley, plopped down 800 yen, accepted four micro bottles of water.

I tipped the first one to the now smiling flight attendant, and emptied it in seconds.

"Do you know that water is critical to support human life?"

She was wilting and smiling at the same time. I kept my lecture short. "If one of these passengers starts choking right now would you give them some water?" I drained the second bottle.

She was good; very, very good. "Sir, water is 200 yen. Cash." I've never seen a more conflicted adherence to misguided corporate policy. I took pity on her and saluted her before guzzling the third bottle.

I completed a couple currency conversion deals, and made a big production of buying six more of the little bottles. What a value! I drank most them before landing. You know how you can be sure you've had enough fluid? When your urine runs clear. That didn't happen until after I'd landed, bought a few two liter bottles of Evian, and sucked one of them dry.

Economy airlines can go too far. In my estimation, this one did. It's called JetStar -- nice people, on-time, and low-cost. Except for the drinks.

RALEIGH, NORTH CAROLINA -- 2015

Eat Your Dog Food

Engineers should try their own design; that is, they should take a bite of their own dog food.

I turned the fan knob down a few notches.

On a deserted midnight highway just outside Raleigh, at 75 miles per hour, my rental car suddenly shuddered and began losing momentum. I looked in the rear-view mirror, because I'd just passed the only other vehicle around, a massive 18-wheeler.

Which was now bearing down on me. Think.

My rental car was brand new, with 553 miles on the glowing, heads-up digital odometer. It was made by one of the big three American auto companies. As I pulled it out of the Avis lot, a mist began forming on the windshield. I'd switched on the defroster and jacked the fan to maximum. It had roared. A powerful fan is a good thing, especially in the steamy, summer nights of the southern United States.

I hit the gas to try and put some distance between my rear bumper and the rapidly closing behemoth truck. Nothing...

There was a second lane, so the situation wasn't dire, but the thought of having passed this poor trucker and then forcing him into the left lane seconds later to pass *me* was not acceptable.

The car continued slowing. The engine RPMs rose toward the redline. I took my foot off the gas. What could be failing? The speedometer dropped below 60, so I gently tried the accelerator a second time. The engine roared. The tachometer, which I might have viewed seconds ago as a gratuitous waste of dash space, showed RPMs ramping above 5,000 yet the car continued to decelerate.

The big headlights behind me loomed closer. I considered pulling onto the shoulder, but there wasn't much room there. I flexed the brake and then the accelerator pedal. Nothing happened, yet the engine was humming. The coincidence of high RPMs and zero torque meant the car had to be out of gear.

The big rig was nearly on my tail. The speedometer read 48. Shifting lights and a loud drone indicated the truck driver had lost patience and he flashed past in the left lane.

"Where's the freaking gear shift on this?" I shouted above the roar of the fan, just because nobody could hear. But really, where?

Why was the fan roaring when I'd just turned it down? Like a mallet-blow to the head, the obvious now struck me. "The fan knob!"

While fumbling for the seat belt a few minutes ago, I had turned a different knob, to first back it out, and then to put it into drive. It was right next to the fan knob, next to the volume knob, next to the tuning knob. The transmission was not "three on the tree," nor was it the more modern axial up-and-down automatic shifter that has reigned, in many variations, for three decades.

Instead, this car's transmission had a knob. Everything was a knob! They were all clustered together like this:

No, Detroit. This is *not* OK.

Later, I studied this carefully. Was the parking brake also an emergency brake? Would pushing it down (or pulling it up?) at speed safely slow the car or destroy the brake and result in wheel-lockup, damage, and spin-out? It turned out that when I checked the online manual later that using this brake for anything but parking was a bad idea. And there was no emergency brake.

Warning, this paragraph is a lecture. An analog control device, like a knob, is not really appropriate to control something so digital as a transmission. This made no sense.

As I ate the dust of the trucker that had roared past me, I shouted something like "What wing-nut engineered this monstrosity!" just because nobody could hear me scream.

I turned the transmission knob from Neutral back to Drive. The car bolted back up to speed. I upped the fan and cleared the windshield, turned the radio knob to find the hardest rock station in North Carolina, and cranked up the volume. Then I passed that poor trucker one more time at 90 mph.

The whole episode made me ask, what does my customer expect from me? If I liked using my product, probably they would too. How to find out? Use it myself before selling it. Eat some of my own dog food. At that particular moment, that sounded tasty.

Broken Star

Politics and celebrity inflame an odd mix of passions.

"He done nuttin' wrong, man!" said one my newest friends, who'd just introduced himself as Evander. His kind smile didn't fade, but his voice had risen sharply. "Why you want to do that?"

My two other new friends and I followed his forceful gesture with his arm and walking stick which he extended as a pointer, nearly hitting a gaggle of teenagers. They politely halted in their tracks, saw there was nothing to see that they hadn't already just stepped away from, and moved on.

Evander's gesture was aimed squarely at the small crowd gathered around the now arson-assaulted star of the then president of the United States.

"Hold on, brother!" said Griffin. Like Evander, he was a black man, but decades younger and dressed to the nines in suit, starched white shirt, and conservative striped tie. Perhaps he wasn't any hotter than some of the costumed movie characters such as Buzz Lightyear and Darth Vader who were around us, but he looked too warm to me for early afternoon on a late July day. "You know he done things, he told us he done things. The man is a sinner."

"Ain't no crime to be a sinner," Evander retorted. "We'ze all sinners."

"Yeah, I know, man, I know," agreed Griffin. "Why you think I'm dressed like this?"

Since nobody seemed to know, I ventured: "Job interview with a financial services company?" For some reason, it was the first thing that sprang to mind connecting the suit with the sin and crime theme.

"No, brother," he responded, "I just went before the judge. I'm a criminal in the eyes of the law."

"What did you do?" asked Miguel.

"I got arrested with a steak knife on me. The judge asked me why I had it, I told him so's I can cut my steak." Miguel and I laughed, but Evander just shook his head. "Considering my prior offenses, the judge was mighty kind to let me off easy."

"You livin' where I live," said Evander, "you better keep that steak knife on ya."

Miguel, who fifteen minutes previously had been the first to introduce himself and thus spontaneously formed our little clique, now spoke up. "He wants to stop everyone except Norwegians from coming to America."

Evander turned to address Miguel in a very direct way. "You guys come here illegal-like, and you take all the jobs. Then when this guy," he pointed back at the broken star, "try'n stop you, it's 'oh, why don't you help us, brothers?'"

"Easy, man, eazzzy!" said Griffin, putting a hand on Evander's shoulder, and using the other to loosen the Windsor knot of his tie, a dual gesture that to me marked him as one of those wise peacemakers who also prepares for battle.

Meanwhile, a few meters away near the crowded broken star, a portly man in a too-small black T-shirt had begun waving an enormous U.S. flag. There had been a nationally televised fight over the star last night, and another one just an hour ago. It turned out, shortly after we left, another fight broke out. This continued for days while the city of Hollywood pondered removing the president's star – or what little was left of it. The counter-argument: where would you stop? Kevin Spacey's star was right next to it, and he wasn't at his peak poll numbers, either, right then.

The portly man with the flag ignored a gathering storm of fist-raising hecklers. The shouts grew louder, and the flag-waver grew more ambitious, nearly falling over in his attempts to reverse the flag's direction. The whole thing made me wonder, but it mostly made me thirsty. It was hot out here on Hollywood Boulevard.

"You know," said Miguel. "He is my president too, but that doesn't mean he is going to help me or my family in any way."

Evander had nothing to say to that. None of us did.

My daughter and her friend from the Czech Republic walked up. They were done shopping and the look on Michelle's face telegraphed, what's all this, dad?

"He's my president, too," I said. "And I reserve my First Amendment right to be critical of his performance."

Evander nodded. He was a smart, worldly man. "You'll see. He'll make you proud."

"He better," said Griffin. "He better make us all proud. You git to be president to do proud, you better do it right."

There was not a thing more to say about that, and the teenagers were eager to see Venice Beach. We all shook hands and parted as friends who had come together briefly next to the broken star.

If you enjoyed this book, leave a review on Amazon, and check out its predecessor:

Missions Accomplished and some funny business along the way

Connect with Tim

missionsaccomplishedpress.com

missionsaccomplished@yahoo.com

http://missions.uniiweb.com/

Amazon Author Page:
https://www.amazon.com/Tim-Jenkins/e/B07B2L9PGN?ref=dbs_p_ebk_r00_abau_000000

Where to next?

Made in the USA
Coppell, TX
07 December 2019

12562107R00155